SEX VERSUS SURVIVAL

John Launer is a doctor, family therapist, educator and writer. He is a well-known columnist for national and international medical journals. He has published five previous books including *How not to be a doctor, and other essays*, commended as a Book of the Year by the British Medical Association. John is on the senior staff at the Tavistock Clinic, the leading training institute in the United Kingdom for psychological treatment. He is also associate dean for postgraduate medical education at London University. John is married to Lee Wax and they have twins, Ruth and David. Details of John's work and writing can be found at http://www.johnlauner.com

SEX VERSUS SURVIVAL

The story of Sabina Spielrein:
her life, her ideas, her genius.

John Launer

Sex versus survival.
The story of Sabina Spielrein:
her life, her ideas, her genius.

Copyright 2011
All Rights Reserved
John Launer
http://www.johnlauner.com

ISBN 978-1-4709-7287-5

Dedicated to the memory of Sabina Spielrein 1885-1942
and her family

CONTENTS

INTRODUCTION

Why is sex so complicated? Why is sexual attraction accompanied by negative feelings like anxiety as well as positive ones like joy? How can we feel attracted to other people even when we don't like them - or even when we know in advance that they won't be any good for us? A hundred years ago, a young Russian woman proposed an answer to these questions. Her name was Sabina Spielrein.

The story of Sabina Spielrein is a remarkable one, on many levels. Born in Tsarist Russia in 1885, she was a victim of childhood abuse by her father and then had a severe breakdown in her teens. She became a psychiatric patient and then had an affair with her psychiatrist, Carl Jung. When this became dangerous for both of them, she got in touch with Jung's colleague and mentor Sigmund Freud, who helped them to disengage and made sure there wasn't a scandal. She qualified as a doctor, became a colleague of Freud and then worked alongside some of the other great figures in psychology in her era. In 1942 she was murdered in the Holocaust, along with her two daughters.

By the time of her death, however, she had vanished from history. For most of the twentieth century the main record of her existence consisted of four footnotes in Freud's essays. When the correspondence between Jung and Freud was published in the 1970s, it showed the dramatic part she had played in bringing the two men together, and then as a cause of their bitter feud. Later, her own diaries and letters came to light in a cardboard box in Geneva. These showed her relationship to the men, in her own words. More documents then emerged, some of her own scholarly papers were republished, and her name became quite well known. People wrote books about her, and produced movies and plays. Now, with the release of 'A Dangerous Method', directed by David Cronenberg and with Keira Knightley in the starring role, Sabina Spielrein has become truly famous.

But there is one story about Sabina Spielrein that remains to be told. It is the most remarkable one of all: she was one of the first people ever to attempt to bridge human psychology with the biology of sexual reproduction. She believed we should understand the human mind in terms of its evolutionary purposes, and in particular the drive to reproduce. She described reproduction as something destructive as well as creative. While it creates a new generation, it also destroys the original identity of both male and female. In our minds, Spielrein said, we know there is a tension between the wish to have sex and the wish to survive. She proposed that these ideas should form the basis of Freud's 'talking cure'.

Freud and Jung rejected Sabina Spielrein's theory in its entirety. They felt it reflected her own mental and sexual problems. They dismissed her as 'the little girl'. They were unable to separate their judgment of her ideas from their personal involvement with her. Over and above their prejudices, the main reason for their dismissal was that Spielrein based her ideas on biology. The world of psychoanalysis was deeply hostile to the kind of biological thinking she put forward. To her critics, both the person and her ideas were pathological. For them, Spielrein *embodied* biology. Their rejection of her theory sealed its fate. Few people have ever read it subsequently. Virtually all those who do read it echo Freud and Jung's criticisms of both the person and her ideas. Literally no-one has assessed her ideas before with a knowledge of modern evolutionary biology, or judged them from that perspective. *Sex versus Survival* does so.

Spielrein herself described her theory as meaning 'more to me than my whole life'. In many ways her ideas were a hundred years ahead of their time. She anticipated some of the major discoveries during the rest of her century. These include the 'selfish gene', the link between sexual reproduction and death, the role of competition and conflict between the sexes in mating, and the field of evolutionary psychology. Not everything she wrote has turned out to be correct: like all her contemporaries, she reached conclusions that were implausible, and mistaken. However taken overall, her biological reasoning pointed towards an approach to the human mind and the talking cure that holds up well in terms of today's knowledge.

A hundred years later, we can stand back, look again at what Spielrein said, and take a more objective view. We have a far better understanding of how the voices and ideas of women, victims of sexual abuse, and those with a psychiatric history, have been ignored. We are in a better position to reassess her ideas, without the same prejudices. We are also better placed to reconsider her approach to the talking cure. The relationship between psychology and biology is now beginning to move in the direction Spielrein might have hoped. In recent years, practicing psychologists and therapists from several different schools of thought have started to become interested in the biological basis of the emotions, and in the evolutionary purposes of how we behave towards each other. Surprisingly, they remain unaware that she came up with similar ideas a century ago. You will find no reference to her in any modern textbook of psychology, nor in any writing about evolution. She may have become famous in our time, but not for the reason she most deserves.

Sex versus Survival is an attempt to evaluate her ideas in the light of today's understanding and to stake a claim for her genius as a thinker. Enormous numbers of people have benefited from Freud's talking cure and all the other talking treatments that have descended from it, including psychotherapy, counseling and coaching. But much has been lost. It is fascinating to think what might have happened if Freud or some of his successors had properly understood how Sabina Spielrein was trying to bridge their world with biology, and followed some of the signposts she offered. It might have led to a unified view of the human mind in which there was no separation of memories, feelings and symptoms from the ideas of variation, natural selection and sexual selection. It might have helped us develop quite different notions of unconscious drives, not as mysterious forces with Latin and Greek names (libido, Oedipus complex and so on) but as biological imperatives that we share with all other sexual animals, and that we have to manage in uniquely human ways. Most important, it might have helped us to understand ourselves as Spielrein proposed: as the creatures of biology, in whom the inescapable facts of sexual reproduction – with all its inherent conflicts – are central to our identity, and a potential source of self-awareness.

In *Sex versus Survival* I weave a factual account of Sabina Spielrein's life together with a presentation and evaluation of her ideas. Readers who prefer to read only her life story will find this in Chapters 1-5 and Chapters 10-14. However I have written this book for the general reader with no specialized knowledge of psychology or biology, while trying to present the ideas in a way that might also convince readers who are knowledgeable in these fields. People who know about evolution often have little awareness of how therapists think, while many people offering talking treatments have scant knowledge of evolutionary biology. I have tried to explain both sets of ideas in a way that might make them intelligible and appealing. I have made a choice not to pepper the text with citations, references or footnotes in the manner of an academic treatise, although there is a guide for further reading at the end of the book. This includes many of the sources of my argument in these pages. I have tried to steer clear of the sectarian controversies that bedevil the worlds of both evolutionary studies and the talking treatments, and can obscure what is important.

Anyone who knows John Kerr's book 'A Dangerous Method' will notice that my account of Spielrein is very different from his. I make use of sources – and ideas – that weren't available when he wrote his book almost twenty years ago. I focus on Spielrein herself rather than the dispute between Jung and Freud. Most important of all, I base my discussion of her ideas on the biological part of her theory, which Kerr doesn't quote, and I examine it in its own biological terms, not in psychoanalytic ones.

In *Sex versus Survival* I do not make the case for a purely biological understanding of psychology, nor vice versa. As a doctor, I take biology seriously. As a therapist I recognize the dangers of naïve biological determinism – and I address these in the course of the book. I acknowledge how culture, language, politics, faith and society all have an influence on what are, and on what we make of ourselves. I also want to emphasize that a biological approach does not in any way imply that monogamous heterosexuality is the 'norm'. Indeed, an evolutionary view sees the range of sexualities to be exactly what they are: variations of strategy to cope with the competing demands of survival and reproduction.

One of the benefits of publishing in the electronic age is that writing a book is no longer like putting a message into a bottle and casting it into the ocean, uncertain who will ever read it or what they will think. *Sex versus Survival* is meant to be the start of a conversation and not its conclusion. I look forward to opportunities for debate and development of the issues I raise. I recognize that the view I offer of Spielrein will be controversial. My aim is the same as Spielrein's: to promote intelligent and critical dialogue between biology and psychology, and an understanding of the human mind that draws on both.

John Launer, November 2011

ONE

Beginnings, childhood, breakdown

Sabina Spielrein came from an exceptional background. In the middle of the nineteenth century her family had been traditional, orthodox Jews. However, by the time Sabina was born they had undergone the kind of social transformation that was common in western Europe, but still rare for Jews in Russia. In one or two generations they moved into the wealthy middle class, and become highly educated and cosmopolitan. They moved freely among their Russian contemporaries and intellectual society. They travelled widely. As we shall see, their views about women and sex were as liberal as anyone in Vienna or Paris.

We know about Sabina Spielrein's family and childhood from diaries she kept in her mid-twenties, and also from the medical notes Jung wrote when she was his patient. Sabina was born on 7 November 1885. Her mother, Eva Lublinskaya, was the daughter and grand-daughter of rabbis. Sabina described her great-grandfather as 'a large, friendly man in black. In our town he was borne through the streets by the people…' From her description, he sounds a remarkable man, something of a local saint. 'He had calmly predicted his death, to the minute', she wrote. 'He did not die but, rather, took his leave of us and went to God.'

Eva's father, Sabina's grandfather, was similar. 'My grandfather loved people', Sabina wrote, 'His house was always open to all comers'. She described how he had suffered a big disappointment in his life: he wanted to marry a Christian woman, the daughter of a physician, but was forbidden to do so. Despite his calling, he clearly followed the enlightenment practices of the west by encouraging secular learning and social assimilation. According to Sabina, he allowed his daughter Eva to go to a Christian high school 'because he considered study of the Christian sciences more important than anything else'. Later, Eva trained as a dentist, although she doesn't seem to have practiced for long. One of her brothers trained as a doctor. By this time the family were settled in Rostov-on-Don, on the Black Sea coast.

Sabina's father was a businessman, a dealer in animal feed. Born originally in Warsaw as Naphthali Spielrein, he moved to Russia and changed his first name to Nikolai. His marriage to Eva was arranged through a family introduction. She had initially resisted it. Like her own father, she had a Christian sweetheart in the past, but she told him she could only marry someone Jewish. According to Sabina, he tragically shot himself. Doomed liaisons with Christians were, it seems, already a tradition in Sabina's family.

Eva's family liked Nikolai for his intelligence and his piety although Sabina described this as a double-edged sword. 'On the one hand', she wrote, 'my father may have had strong religious feeling that takes the form of a destiny-like force, perhaps also in a sense of calling, but in the eyes of the "true believers" my father is a downright heretic.' She was also sure her parents' marriage was not a happy one: 'My mother did not find satisfaction in love for her husband', she wrote.

Sabina had three younger brothers – Jacob, Isaac and Emil – who were all to become distinguished scientists. The youngest child was another girl, Emilia. Their upbringing was materially comfortable, and intellectually ambitious. Eva and Nikolai had clearly done well. They lived in a lavish house, a 'sugar-cake style' rococo palace on one of Rostov's principal streets. At the age of five Sabina was sent to stay with family in Warsaw to the Froebel Kindergarten. Later, back in Russia, she learned to speak German and English fluently, as well as French: a matter of course for children of their social class in Russia. 'Papa speaks French with me and Jascha (Jacob), and German with Sanja (Isaac)' she wrote. In addition, Sabina chose to learn biblical Hebrew 'so as to read the Bible in the original'. The family had many servants, and employed both a music teacher and a private tutor. The Spielrein family took holidays in Switzerland, Germany and elsewhere.

Sabina was an imaginative child. At the age of three or four she dug holes in the ground to find out what was on the other side of the globe. According to a later diary, she tried to make a baby by mixing together different materials. 'I spread leftover food and drink on the table', she wrote, then carefully mixed it all together, making a great mess, because I wanted to see what would come out of it. It gave me great joy when one color changed into another or a new form or consistency resulted…I had a lot of little bottles with "secret" liquids, "magic stones" and the like, from which I was expecting "the great creation". ' From the age of seven or eight, she had an imaginary guardian spirit with whom she held conversations. But there was more troubled play as well. For example, she would sit on the floor, with her heel against her anus, trying to defecate and prevent herself doing so at the same time, as a form of arousal.

Sabina wrote about both her parents with affection and respect. 'Fundamentally', she recorded, 'I feel that I have an unusually good, wholly unselfish father, to whom I owe much gratitude'. It is clear that her parents were passionate, articulate, well-read and broad-minded people. However it is equally clear that the emotional climate of the household was very troubled. A note from Jung in her later hospital records gives an impression of the kinds of arguments that went on:

'Her mother has the odd habit of having to buy everything she sees and can be talked into buying: every time she goes out shopping she brings home masses of things that are very expensive. She never has enough money on her to pay for everything and therefore has to borrow from relatives and then struggle to repay them from her household budget. Above all father must not know about this, so there is constant anxiety that father might find out about these dealings. From time to time when father gets a whiff of what is going on there is a huge row'.

Eva Spielrein had affairs with other men – while insisting that Sabina herself was kept ignorant about sex. Sabina's father was prone to suicidal depression and suffered outbursts of rage. Sometimes he would punish Sabina by smacking her on her buttocks, doing this in front of her siblings in order to humiliate her. On one occasion she begged him not to beat her, as he was trying to lift her skirt from behind. He gave in, but forced her to kneel down and kiss a picture of her grandfather and to swear always to be a good child.

Spielrein experienced a sense of loneliness. In addition to her guardian spirit, she invented an imaginary friend, a young Jewish girl who would be the brightest in the class. Then 'such a girl actually turned up' at Sabina's school. 'I loved her with all the intensity of childish love. That lasted a while (one year). Then I became somewhat disappointed in her and chose a Christian girl as my best friend.'

In spite of her father's agnosticism, Sabina was extremely religious to the age of thirteen. She then acquired an interest in science, and was determined to become a doctor, like one of her uncles. Her maternal grandfather, Rabbi Mark Lublinsky, inevitably gave his approval. It chimed with his enlightened, modern attitude to learning. 'I believe no-one could have been happier than my grandfather', she wrote, 'when I decided to study medicine'.

Sabina did well academically at high school, but in spite of this she developed problems that we would regard as signs of mental illness – apathy, tics, and psychosomatic ailments including stomach problems. She developed a crush on her history teacher: 'I wanted to make some sacrifices for him. I wanted to suffer for him', she wrote. She had vivid sexual fantasies, many involving punishment or defecation. When she was sixteen, her only sister Emilia died at the age of six, suddenly, from typhoid. This was devastating. 'I withdrew completely from other people', she wrote later in her diary. 'After the death of my little sister, my illness began. I took refuge in isolation and left my two girl friends to become best friends'. She became moody, difficult and at times agitated. Her family sent her to stay with relatives in Warsaw. There, her mental condition deteriorated further.

In the early summer of 1904, her mother and a maternal uncle, Dr Lublinsky, took her to Interlaken in Switzerland, to a sanatorium specializing in mental disorders. Her admission there for four weeks was not a success. Next, they took her to the outpatient clinic at the University of Zurich, run by an eminent Russian, Professor Monakov. However he considered her too disturbed for treatment there. Finally, on the evening of 17 August 1904, in a state of extreme agitation, and accompanied by her uncle and a medical police official, she was taken to a place of safety. It would bring her into contact with some of the most radical doctors and thinkers of the age, changing her life – and theirs too.

TWO

The patient

The place where she had arrived was probably the safest place in Europe, perhaps in the whole world, for her to be. It was a mental hospital called the Burghölzli, on the outskirts of Zurich. Its founder was Auguste Forel, a pioneer of psychiatry who had turned it into a centre of international repute. At the time Sabina arrived, it was directed by the visionary psychiatrist Eugen Bleuler. His beliefs, and the principles on which he organized the care of patients, were highly enlightened. They anticipated much that we now regard as good care for the mentally ill. 'The most important tools for treating the psyche' he argued, 'are patience, calm and inner goodwill towards the patients, three qualities that must be absolutely inexhaustible'. At the core of Bleuler's approach was the idea that a mental hospital should be a therapeutic community. Every patient, as well as all the staff members and their wives, contributed to the best of their ability. One of Bleuler's disciples later described how 'the spirit of unconditional acceptance of the person, of the healthy as well as the sick, reigned in the hospital'.

Bleuler did not take direct charge of Sabina Spielrein's care. Instead, he handed this over to his deputy, Carl Jung. A large, handsome, boisterous and passionate man, Jung was the son of a Protestant pastor but he already had the makings of a great psychiatrist. Now aged only 29, Jung was at the beginning of his career and had married into a wealthy family. Two years previously he had received his doctorate, with a dissertation 'On the psychology and pathology of so-called occult phenomena'. He had not yet met Freud, although he had read much of Freud's published work. Bleuler was encouraging him to try out the approach to mental illness that Freud had described. Sabina Spielrein was therefore to become first patient to undergo psychoanalysis with Jung.

On her admission to the Burghölzli, Jung had not been able to take a proper medical history. The uncle who accompanied her was evidently unhelpful, even though he was himself a doctor. 'As an old Russian Jew,' Jung wrote, 'he constantly gave quite meager and evasive answers, and in addition did not have a good mastery of German'. Perhaps we can take Jung's account at face value, but there may have been other reasons for him to be so negative, including racial prejudice.

In spite of Dr Lublinsky's reticence, Jung clearly managed to elicit some information, perhaps from medical notes that the uncle had brought along with him. On the cover sheet of her file he recorded that Sabina's father was said to be 'Healthy, active, irritable, overwrought, neurasthenic, hot tempered to the point of madness'. After writing this, Jung deleted the word: 'Healthy', suggesting perhaps that Dr Lublinsky gave one version of the story but the previous notes gave a different one. Her mother was described as 'Nervous (like patient), *hysterical?* Is a dentist. Has hysterical absences of a childish nature.' Following Bleuler's guidance, Jung prescribed strict bed rest, protection from all distractions, no visits, and regular conversations with her doctor according to Freud's method.

The conversations with Jung would not nowadays be classed as psychoanalysis. He was untrained in the method, and the techniques were too haphazard. Once a day, for several months, Jung visited Sabina for a consultation, spending up to three hours at a time with her. He encouraged her to talk, especially about her past experiences, and to remember what had happened to her. His approach was based on the Freudian principle of 'anamnesis' – learning to recall significant and traumatic events from earlier life by speaking without any guidance or interruption. He also used his own method of word association. This involved tracing a particular pattern in people's psychological make-up – a so-called 'complex' – through asking them to give quick and instinctive responses to certain words without having time to reflect.

Luckily, we have hospital records containing a detailed account of Spielrein's problems and treatment. They include thirteen pages of Jung's notes and two entries by Bleuler, as well as correspondence with Spielrein's parents. We also have further accounts relating to this time. These include Jung's subsequent letters to Freud, and also Jung's published case histories: it is often easy to work out from these which of his patients he is describing.

After her admission to the Burghölzli, Spielrein behaved with a level of disturbance that we would certainly regard as highly hysterical. Some historians have even suggested she had schizophrenia, although this seems most unlikely. 'Patient laughs and cries in a strangely mixed, compulsive manner', Jung wrote. 'Masses of tics, she rotates her head jerkily, sticks out her tongue, twitches her legs.' The next day there was a 'constant alternation of laughter and tears, jerking of the head, seductive glances.'

Accounts of this kind of hysterical behaviour in psychiatric patients were far commoner at the time than now. Some of Freud's case histories, and those from other contemporary psychiatrists, are similar, particularly relating to young women. It seems that hysteria of this nature was one of the few ways available for women from oppressive backgrounds to express their distress in a way that would be taken seriously and attract attention and help.

In the weeks following her admission, Spielrein made suicide threats, hid knives, and left a ladder and benches as obstacles for people to fall over. She was openly masochistic. 'She constantly demands that the writer inflict pain on her', Jung wrote, 'do something to hurt her, treat her badly in some way; we are never merely to ask something of her, but to command it.'

Later he would write about this to Freud: 'Any situation which reflected violence aroused her, for example being told to obey. As soon as she was alone she would imagine all kinds of torments; the same things happened in her dreams: for example, she often dreamt that she was eating her lunch and simultaneously sitting on the lavatory and that everything was going straight out through her bottom; at the same time she was surrounded by a large crowd of people watching her; on another occasion she was being whipped in front of a great mob of people etc.'

At first, Jung's conversations with her took place only in her room, where she was confined. Later, they took walks together in the hospital grounds. Jung describes an revealing occasion on one of these walks, when she accidentally dropped her cloak. He picked it up and began to beat the dust out of it with a stick. She tore the cloak from him. It had aroused both her sexual excitement and her anger.

Her behaviour in the hospital was erratic. At the end of September, Jung wrote an entry in her notes as follows: 'The states of excitation have become less frequent recently. Patient still uses her unoccupied hours for her childish pranks (suicidal gestures to drive the nurses crazy, running away, hiding, giving people scares, transgressing prohibitions.) After these excesses, sometimes a severe depressive reaction. Patient has great insight into her condition but not the slightest inclination to improve it'.

Impressively, Spielrein had made a considerable recovery by the end of 1904. Jung's treatment was clearly making a difference. However she had also become more sexual in her attitude to Jung. 'Patient now shows more initiative and demands regular useful activities,' Jung recorded in his notes. 'Yesterday at my evening visit patient was reclining on the sofa in her usual oriental, voluptuous manner, with a sensuous, dreamy expression on her face'.

In addition to Jung's treatment, Bleuler's involvement had also helped her to get better. He wrote numerous letters to her father, effectively banning him from any contact with her: 'Your daughter needs to develop independence and self-reliance and must therefore remain unencumbered by all emotional anxiety for her family and all restricting aspects of family life.' The Swiss historian Angela Graf-Nold argues that Bleuler's care for Spielrein was in fact more consistent than Jung's, and possibly played the greater part in her recovery: 'What was unusual in Sabina Spielrein's case', Graf-Nold writes, 'was how unreservedly Bleuler stood up for her: she could rely on his unwavering backing for her apparently almost hopeless struggle for independence from her father and from her whole family by whom she felt literally "possessed." '

Some writers have suggested that Mr. Spielrein may in fact have perpetrated sexual abuse on his daughter as well as physical abuse, and that Bleuler perhaps suspected this. Spielrein's own positive comments about her father in her diary, and her eventual return to be near him in Russia, make this seem improbable. Nonetheless, the boundary between his physical humiliation of her and overt sexual activity may be debatable.

In keeping with the philosophy of the hospital, Spielrein started to attend clinical and theoretical lectures, alongside the staff and the less disturbed patients. Within a few months, Jung invited her to become his research assistant for the remainder of her time at the Burghölzli, helping him with his work on word association. He lent books to her, and encouraged her to revive her ambitions to study medicine. 'Minds like your help to advance science', he told her. 'You must become a psychiatrist'. By April 1905, Bleuler felt she was sufficiently stable for him to recommend her as a medical student. She was discharged from the Burghölzli in June, and started her university studies the next semester. Her psychological recovery had been swift and remarkable by any standards.

However, one significant problem remained: the feelings she had developed for Jung. She had told her mother about this, and Mrs. Spielrein asked Jung to send her to a different psychiatrist. Jung wrote a referral letter to Freud. He described her case in some detail: 'She initially harassed everybody, tormenting the nurses to the limit of their endurance. As the analysis progressed, her condition noticeably improved and she finally emerged as a highly intelligent and talented person of great sensibility. There is a certain callousness and unreasonableness in her character and she lacks any feeling for situation and external propriety, but much of this must be put down to Russian peculiarities.'

He concluded the letter: 'During treatment the patient had the misfortune to fall in love with me. She raves on to her mother about her love in an ostentatious manner, and a secret perverse enjoyment of her mother's dismay seems to play a not inconsiderable part. In view of this situation, her mother therefore wishes, if the necessity arises, to place her elsewhere for treatment, with which I am naturally in agreement.'

Jung sent the letter to Mrs. Spielrein so that she could forward it to Freud in Vienna if she wished. Freud never received it. We have to assume that for some reason Mrs. Spielrein decided not to send the letter on to him. Perhaps Sabina persuaded her not to, so that she could continue to see the doctor she loved. Jung did not make any further attempts to send her elsewhere for treatment, in spite of knowing about her strong feelings for him. He continued to see her as a patient for four more years, but in his home rather than at the Burghölzli. He did not ask her to pay fees for this, even though he knew how wealthy her family were. Later, this fact was to lead to some highly significant exchanges between Jung, Spielrein, her mother, and Freud.

THREE

Medical student and mistress

During the years from 1905 to 1910 Sabina Spielrein was a medical student. 'Hell!' she wrote, on her first day at medical school. 'I've been to the university. Such a mountain of impressions that I haven't the patience to describe them. I liked the professor of Zoology, Lange very much'. We know from records that she attended lectures during the years that followed in botany, osteology, (the study of bones), physical anthropology, genetics and behaviour among other subjects. In vacations there were trips back to Rostov, and sometimes her parents or uncle from Warsaw also visited her in Zurich.

She rented a room in a part of Zurich known as the 'Russian colony'. Many émigré Russians lived there. Some were poor, including revolutionary exiles who were the focus of local prejudice. Others, including many of the young women, were wealthier and had come to Switzerland to pursue studies that might not have been possible for them in Russia. They concentrated on their courses and kept away from politics. One of these was a woman called Vera Chatzmann: she later married a chemist from Manchester called Chaim Weizmann, who was to become the first president of Israel.

Spielrein continued as Jung's patient. We can trace the development of their relationship from a medical one to a friendship mainly through her diaries, her letters to her mother and Jung's letters to her. Sadly, her own letters to him from this period haven't survived.

The first of Spielrein's diaries that exists is from around 1905-7, when she was still in the early years of medical school. There are three surviving extracts, taking the form of a long imaginary debate with Jung about the nature of sex and love. Possibly they were intended as a letter to him. The debate in them is intricate, personal and passionate. They show her struggling to formulate her own ideas about sex, and how these are intertwined with her thoughts about Jung. They testify to her strong feeling for him, but there is nothing in them that suggests sex is as yet anything more than a discussion topic at this stage: 'We must not forget the fundamental difference between man and woman', Spielrein wrote. 'Man wants to embrace, woman prefers to be embraced. Woman is more discriminating in her choice because it is more difficult to find a personality that fits the ideal. It is for these reasons that the woman is generally monogamous when she truly loves; for opposite reasons, the man is less discriminating and more or less polygamous.'

The pages also contain some of the ideas she was later to develop into her theory. 'Every individual must disappear as such,' she states. 'In the case of an amoeba the whole 'personality' in fact literally disappears; in the case of a human being only a fraction disappears. But the instinct is always of death, the annihilation of the personality, two individuals fused into one…This is also how the resistance of every personality to the sexual instinct can be explained. I do not imply here that two people who feel a sexual attraction to each other wish to be constantly fused into one union or anything like that…Sexual feeling is always tamed by other feelings even during the sexual act, otherwise you would be facing a passionate killer or a martyr. I mean that, by destroying, a man wants to annihilate himself while the woman wants to be annihilated.'

In one passage she describes how she is thinking about certain aspects of love to see how they fit in with the purpose of procreation. Although her writing is convoluted, it seems that she is trying unsuccessfully to persuade Jung about how everything is related to reproduction. 'Why does love exist and not coarse sexual attraction?' she wrote. 'How can sexual feeling be diverted into something else, or rather, how does this conform to the view that everything tends to promote to preservation of the species? I beg you, do not be impatient straight away. I do not want you to take this the wrong way. There is a fundamental difference between your concept and mine, and if we are not in agreement, I will not be able to prove to you why some phenomenon or other seems to me to have a difference cause, and that torments me.'

As she progressed through medical school, and continued to visit Jung as her psychiatrist, it is clear that boundaries between them as doctor and patient became blurred. She became one of Jung's most ardent students. Spielrein kept her mother informed of her evolving relationship with her private doctor, and did so with surprising frankness. Meanwhile, Jung continued to send reports to Spielrein's mother in Rostov as he might with any private patient.

However, he also started to confide in Spielrein about the limitations of his marriage, and about the perceived deficiencies of his wife Emma. Increasingly, they shared intimate thoughts about psychology, poetry, religion, mythology, literature and music. Attracted by his dark, Jewish, impulsive Russian patient, he gradually began to get drawn into an elaborate fantasy she had created about an imagined son named Siegfried, an ambiguous mental creation that at times seemed to represent 'a heroic destiny' for which she was willing to sacrifice herself, and at other times the flesh and blood child of a prospective union between them.

Jung's letters from that time, and Spielrein's reflections written afterwards, paint a picture of a relationship of Wagnerian intensity, involving two people who were entirely different in their cultural and religious backgrounds, but alike in their extraordinary intelligence and passionate emotionality. There seems little doubt that by 1908 Jung and Spielrein were engaged in physical contact. There is much mention of 'poetry', in contexts that do not sound like textual study or recitation. During the same period, Jung's professional relationship with Freud took off, and the letters between the two men also share the same sense of creativity and excitement. In one of his first letters to Freud, he reported on his 'difficult case, a young Russian girl student, ill for six years.' He also talked about his 'case' at a conference in Amsterdam where he presented Freud's ideas. He didn't mention on either occasion that she had recovered, was now at medical school, was seeing him in his own house, and was becoming intimate with him.

From hints, it seems fair to guess that on some occasions in 1907-8 they reached mutual orgasm together, through what we might now call heavy petting. In the days before effective contraception, it would probably have been too hazardous for them to risk full intercourse. There is no suggestion that Jung was drawn into enacting Spielrein's beating fantasies, although these may well have been passing through her own mind.

Throughout their affair, Jung was frank with Spielrein about his view of marriage, and about his own need for polygamy. 'I must tell you briefly what a lovely impression I received of you today,' he wrote. 'You have no idea how much it means to me, to be able to love someone I do not have to condemn to the banality of habit, and who does not condemn herself to that fate.' As Spielrein soon became aware, she was not his only mistress at the time, and he had many more during his long life. He had come to believe that his own marriage – indeed all marriage – was a lie: a consequence of sexual desire but also a cause of its inevitable loss.

It is worth noting that Jung's view of marriage was not a great deal different from Freud's. Indeed, Freud had already confessed to Jung that his own marriage was 'amortized': in other words like a loan that had been fully paid off. On another occasion, Freud made his views even clearer by describing his relationship with his wife as 'not a bad solution of the marriage problem.'

Jung's passion for Spielrein's was interspersed with intervals of remorse. 'My dear,' he wrote in December 1908, 'I regret so much. I regret my weaknesses and curse the fate that is threatening me...Will you forgive me for being as I am? For offending you with being like this, for forgetting my duties as a doctor towards you? Will you understand that I am one of the weakest and most unstable of human beings? And will you never take revenge on me for that, either in words, or in thoughts or feelings? I am looking for someone who understands how to love, without punishing the other person, imprisoning him or sucking him dry; I am seeking this as yet unrealized person who will make it possible that love can be independent of social advantage and disadvantage, so that love may always be an end in itself, and not just a means to an end'. Spielrein was blunt in her reply: 'You are trying to suppress all the stronger feelings you have towards me. As a result you are surviving on mere diplomacy and lies'.

She told almost no-one about what was going on. However, she continued to write to her mother as the relationship developed: 'Let us say, his wife is not completely satisfactory and now he has fallen in love with me, a hysteric; and I have fallen in love with a psychopath…An uneven dynamic character coupled with a highly developed sensibility… So far we have remained at the level of poetry that is not dangerous, and we shall remain at that level, perhaps until the time I will become a doctor, unless circumstances will change.' She also indicated that she one day hoped to have his child.

The affair ended in a sensational crisis. Around the end of 1908 someone (probably Jung's wife) wrote to Spielrein's mother to tell her Jung was ruining her daughter. Eva Spielrein contacted Jung begging him not to exceed the bounds of friendship with Sabina. Rumors also began to circulate around Zurich that Jung was having an affair, and word of this eventually reached Freud, although confusingly they related to another woman that Jung wasn't actually seeing.

Jung broke off his affair with Spielrein. He appears to have suffered tremendous swings in his moods. He wrote a furious letter to Eva Spielrein, demanding money for having seen her daughter, if she wanted him to behave like a doctor and not a friend. He resigned his post at the Burghölzli. His declared reason was to develop his private practice, but it seems probable that he was preparing himself for exposure and disgrace at the hospital.

Events then descended into a confused tragi-comedy. Spielrein confronted Jung, only to receive a 'sermon' from him on how she 'wanted too much because he was too good to me etc.' She boxed his ears and assaulted him with a knife. 'I described the manner of our parting to my mother,' she wrote in her diary 'and she passed it along to my father, who said only "People have made a god out of him and he is nothing but an ordinary human being. I am so glad she boxed his ears! I would have done it myself. Just let her do what she thinks necessary: she can take care of herself".'

In spite of her father's sentiments, Spielrein's mother now travelled from Russia intending to confront Jung in person. Jung managed to avoid her. Eva Spielrein had planned to go and see Professor Bleuler to spill the beans. For unknown reasons, she never did. Perhaps her daughter talked her out of it, for fear of destroying Jung's marriage and his career. Unless more documents come to light, we will never know.

FOUR

Between Jung and Freud

From March to July 1909 there was a three-way exchange of letters between Jung, Freud and Spielrein about these events. They provide us with a detailed account of the crisis and its resolution. They also set the scene for the men's later opinions about Spielrein, when the subject under discussion was no longer the affair but her theory.

Jung began the correspondence. Under the mistaken impression that it was Spielrein who was spreading rumors about him, he wrote to Freud: 'a woman patient whom years ago I pulled out of a very sticky neurosis with the greatest devotion, has violated my confidence in the most mortifying way imaginable. She has kicked up a vile scandal solely because I denied myself the pleasure of giving her a child.' He did not say who the woman was. He said nothing about what had actually happened between them. Nor did he tell Freud he had resigned from the Burghölzli that same day.

Freud bought into the deception: 'To be slandered and scorched by the love with which we operate', he replied, 'such are the perils of our trade, which we are certainly not going to abandon on their account.' This might have been the end of the matter, except that Spielrein contacted Freud herself, asking to see him on a matter 'of greatest importance'. Freud assumed this must be the woman slandering Jung, and sent her letter on to him: 'Weird! What is she? A busybody, a chatterbox or a paranoiac?'

Jung replied by telegram and then by letter. He confirmed that he believed Spielrein was the patient spreading rumors about him. He also disclosed she was the 'case' he had described to Freud some years previously: 'She was, so to speak, my test case, for which reason I remembered her with special affection and gratitude. Since I knew from my experience that she would relapse if I withdrew my support, I felt myself morally obliged, as it were, to devote a large measure of friendship to her, until I saw that an unintended wheel had started turning, whereupon I finally broke with her. She was, of course, systematically planning my seduction, which I considered inopportune. Now she is seeking revenge.'

Freud put Spielrein off, and he reassured Jung: 'After receiving your wire I wrote Fraulein Sp a letter in which I affected ignorance, pretending to think her suggestion was that of an over-zealous enthusiast,' He added: 'The way these women manage to charm us with every conceivable psychic perfection until they have attained their purpose is one of nature's greatest spectacles.'

Spielrein now sent Freud more information about why she wanted to see him. 'Four and a half years ago Dr Jung was my doctor,' she wrote, 'then he became my friend and finally my "poet" i.e., my beloved. Eventually he came to me and things went as they usually do with "poetry". He preached polygamy, his wife was supposed to have no objection etc. etc.' She enclosed a letter from Jung displaying his passion for her.

Freud was unmoved by this evidence. He replied: 'Dr Jung is my friend and colleague, I know him in other respects as well, and have reason to believe that he is incapable of frivolous or ignoble behaviour. I am reluctant to set myself up as judge in matters that affect him intimately... I would urge you to ask yourself whether the feelings that have outlived this close relationship are not best suppressed and eradicated, from your own psyche I mean, and without external intervention and the involvement of third persons... PS I am returning the indiscreet enclosure and can only say that I do not hold the somewhat gushing effusion against the young man, although as his senior I have to smile at such appraisals.'

Meanwhile he continued to keep Jung in the picture: 'My reply to her was ever so wise and penetrating,' he wrote. 'I made it appear as though the most tenuous of clues had enabled me, Sherlock Holmes-like, to guess the situation (which of course was none too difficult after her communications) and suggested a more appropriate procedure'. He then added more reassurance: 'In view of the kind of matter we work with, it will never be possible to avoid little laboratory explosions. Maybe we didn't slant the test tube enough, or we heated it too quickly. In this way we learn what part of the danger lies in the matter and what part in our way of handling it.' He offered to forward to Jung the letter she had sent him.

Spielrein finally wrote another letter to Freud – a long, impassioned one that took her several days to write. The draft covers around twenty pages, although it isn't clear if she sent it all. This time she enclosed further correspondence including five letters that Jung had written to her mother offering a variety of excuses, denials and insults. She made it clear that she wasn't seeking revenge, but asking for Freud's intercession so that she and her lover could part as friends.

She didn't wait for a reply. By now she had taken matters into her own hands. She went to see Jung and managed to convince him she wasn't the person spreading rumors about him. Jung sent Freud a confession, of sorts: 'I took too black a view of things. After breaking with her I was almost certain of her revenge and was deeply disappointed by the banality of the form it took. The day before yesterday she turned up at my house and had a *very decent* talk with me, during which it transpired that the rumor buzzing about me does not emanate from her at all.' He admitted his own sexual feeling for her, although implying he had only just realised this: 'I imputed all the other wishes and hopes entirely to my patient without seeing the same thing in myself'.

Without actually describing if anything had happened physically between them, he moved straight on to recent events: 'When the situation had become so tense that the continued perseveration of the relationship could only be rounded out by sexual acts, I defended myself in a manner that cannot be justified morally…I wrote to her mother that I was not the gratifier of her daughter's sexual desires but merely her doctor, and she should free me from her'. He reported that he and Spielrein had now parted as friends: 'She has freed herself from the transference in the best and nicest way and has suffered no relapse (apart from a paroxysm of weeping after the separation).'

Jung ended by asking Freud, as a favour, if he could write to Spielrein making it clear that 'I have fully informed you of the matter, and especially of the letter to her parents which is what I regret the most. I would like to give my patient at least this satisfaction: that you and she would know of my "perfect honesty".'

Freud did write to Spielrein, but in circumspect terms. He did not comply with Jung's chief request, namely to mention his regret over the letter to her parents: 'I have today learned something from Dr Jung himself about the subject of your proposed visit to me, and now I see that I had divined some matters correctly but that I had construed others wrongly and to your disadvantage. I must ask your forgiveness on this latter count. However the fact that I was wrong and that the lapse has to be blamed on the man and not the woman, as my young friend himself admits, satisfies my need to hold women in high regard. Please accept this expression of my entire sympathy for the dignified way in which you have resolved the conflict.'

He then wrote back to Jung: 'Immediately after receiving your letter I wrote Fraulein Sp a few amiable lines and today received an answer from her. Amazingly awkward – is she a foreigner by any chance? – or very inhibited, hard to read and hard to understand. All I can gather from her is that the matter means a great deal to her and that she is very much in earnest. Don't find fault with yourself for drawing me into it: it was not your doing but hers.'

He then offered a benediction: 'I cannot possibly be angry and can only marvel at the profound coherence of all things in this world.' He didn't mention that Spielrein's letters to him had spelled out a great deal that Jung hadn't told him, including the fact that he was her lover, and Jung's outrageous demand for her mother to pay fees.

It was Spielrein who had the last word. She hadn't been taken in by the men's subterfuge, nor by their mutual and self-deceit. She wrote to Freud, in a manner that is astonishing in its directness, and in its perceptiveness about both men and their failings: 'If he were capable of being honest with himself, how happy I should be! Ah, but you are a sly one, Professor Freud… you should have agreed to see me without putting up the slightest resistance. But one likes to spare oneself unpleasant moments. Right? Even the great "Freud" cannot always ignore his own weaknesses.'

FIVE

Lessons

Many historians, writing about this whole episode, have been deeply critical of Jung for his actions and deceit. Some are critical of Freud too for covering up Jung's behaviour. The German feminist historian Sabine Richerbächer described the episode as 'a shabby game.' She wrote: 'Out of calculating power politics, and in an endeavor to avoid any public scandal around psychoanalysis, Freud and Jung together draw up a design to checkmate the queen...She is led up the garden path, pathologised, appeased.'

But not everyone agrees. The American psychoanalyst Zvi Lothane remarks that 'some commentators have previously viewed both Jung's and Freud's handling of the situation as less than honest', but he makes it clear that he dissents. 'The positive lesson of the Jung-Spielrein relationship', he writes, 'is that both protagonists have exemplified and taught us the importance of reciprocal, realistic, objective, altruistic love as an essential ingredient in the therapeutic alliance and in analytic treatment'. Readers will form their own judgments.

One thing is certain: Spielrein conducted herself with more dignity than either of the two men. It is tempting to wonder what might have happened to psychoanalysis if had she behaved in a less measured way. The movement was already under scrutiny in a number of places, including Switzerland. Some people regarded psychoanalysis as an immoral activity. If she had provoked a scandal, it would certainly have ruined Jung's career. It could have damaged Freud as well, and might have imperiled the future of psychoanalysis itself. In the event, her choice of public inaction and private introspection was an important one, for herself and for the emerging psychoanalytic movement.

In the summer of 1909, Spielrein visited her parents in Russia as she generally did during vacations. She had some frank conversations with them about what had happened, but it was some time before she wrote to Jung. This clearly worried him, as his reply showed. It suggests he was also being careful to keep the correspondence private: 'My Dear', he wrote to Spielrein, 'Your letter gave me much pleasure and set my mind at rest. I was rather worried on account of your long silence. I was afraid something had happened to you, or that somehow the devil had a hand in it. There are lovely things in your letter. I must admire your parents' truly great broadmindedness. For a mother, that is a really high achievement and one hardly to be expected. Tell your mother that I admire her for that. It will be easier for your father, for new outlooks and new life values come more readily to a man of ideas than to the natural conservatism of a woman…It will be better if you continue to send your letters to the Burghölzli; someone will send them on to me from there.'

For a while Spielrein contemplated a move to Heidelberg in Germany to complete her studies. Bleuler wrote her a reference. Then she changed her mind. It appears she wanted to remain in Switzerland to resolve matters. She started to practice therapy with schizophrenic patients in the university clinic where she had been turned down as a patient not so many years previously. She continued to visit Jung, but their relationship simmered down. He took over from Bleuler as the supervisor for her final dissertation at medical school – on a case of schizophrenia. Jung arranged for its publication in the 'Yearbook', the journal of the psychoanalytic movement, which he edited.

Spielrein kept a diary intermittently for three years from the summer of 1909, just after the crisis was over. They contain a mixture of day-to-day events, reflections, reminiscences, descriptions of her continuing encounters with Jung, and explicit attempts to make sense of them. Her entries testify to a fluctuating adjustment to the end of their affair. The emotions between them were clearly unequal, more adolescent on her side and now more reserved on his, although there were still moments of intimacy. In September 1910 she wrote in her diary: 'My friend said we would always have to be careful not to fall in love again; we would be dangerous to each other. He admitted to me that so far he knew no female who could replace me. It was as if he had a necklace in which all his other admirers were – pearls, and I – the medallion…At the end he pressed my hand to his heart several times and said this should mark the beginning of a new era. What could he have meant by this?'

In December 1910, just before she sat her finals at medical school, she reported taking part in "the tenderest poetry" with him, followed by ecstatic kissing. This may have been the last occasion it happened, although she went on ruminating in her diaries for some while longer about the relationship, and about what might have been.

All three of the main protagonists in this episode learned significant lessons from it. All of them used the experience to formulate crucial theoretical ideas. The main lesson for Freud was about patients and analysts falling in love with each other. He already knew that patients could be attracted to analysts. He saw this as an example of how patients transferred childhood sexual wishes on to their analysts, calling this 'transference'. However, he now realised that the analysts themselves might be drawn into the same process, and enact their own sexual desires as well: so-called 'counter-transference'. On this basis, he soon insisted that analysts themselves underwent analysis, in order to experience such emotions and gain mastery over them.

The lesson that Jung learned was a different one. His dramatic success in treating Spielrein's symptoms had originally turned him into an enthusiastic Freudian. It convinced him that Freud was right in claiming that sexual fantasies from early childhood lay behind mental disturbance, and that the method of 'free association' was an effective technique in uncovering these. It propelled him towards Freud, and in a short space of time into becoming a close friend and Freud's heir apparent.

However, not long afterwards, the experience led to an entirely different way of thinking. Reflecting on his affair with Spielrein, Jung came up with his central idea that each man or woman held in their mind a so-called 'anima' or 'animus'. This was a deeply buried image of a desired counterpart from the opposite sex, unattainable in reality but open to discovery through analysis and experience. These images, he believed, drew not just on memories from childhood but on visions inspired by religion and mythology, and revealed by art and literature. They were held in the unconscious minds not just of individuals but also of whole societies, cultures and races. Ideas like these were to preoccupy him for the rest of his long life, but they also served to alienate Freud, who considered them to be mystical bunkum. Sabina Spielrein was thus a catalyst for the meeting of minds between Jung and Freud, but also for their subsequent split.

Once she had qualified as a doctor, Spielrein moved to Munich to study art history and music for a few months. She sent Jung the draft of a paper she was writing on sex and death. He didn't find the time to read it properly. In the end she had to ask more than once for him to return it so she could work on it further. She also feared he would steal her ideas for a book he was writing himself, which in fact he later did, although in a garbled form.

In the autumn of 1911 Spielrein went on to Vienna to pursue her medical career. In October she finally met Freud, who admitted her to the Vienna Psychoanalytic Society. She was only its second woman member. Freud invited her to present a lecture to the society the following month. She decided she would present the paper on sex and death that she had worked on since leaving medical school. She intended it as her major contribution to psychoanalysis.

SIX

Sex and death

The Vienna Psychoanalytic Society met monthly in a hired hall and it was there, on the evening 29th of November, 1911, that Spielrein delivered her lecture. Its title was 'Destruction as the Cause of Coming into Being'. Spielrein stated her case very briefly in the first three pages, followed by a lengthy elaboration. Later she worked on the transcript of the lecture to make it suitable for publication as a paper, which happened the following year.

She began on a highly personal note: 'Throughout my involvement with sexual problems', she wrote, 'one question has always fascinated me: why does this most powerful drive, the reproductive instinct, harbor negative feelings in addition to the inherently anticipated positive ones?'

The opening phrase is in itself fascinating. Was she talking about her own sexual problems, her limited clinical experience, or both? It is unclear, but people's perceptions at the time were that she was largely talking about herself. They were probably correct. It was the fashion at the time to mix theoretical speculation with implicit or even explicit personal disclosure. While it might nowadays appear inappropriate or embarrassing to do so, the study of psychology could never have advanced without the courage of some of its pioneers to share their own experiences in this way. However her starting point was certainly interesting from both a psychological and biological point of view: why are we ambivalent about sex?

Spielrein then described some of the existing theories to explain the anxiety that surrounds sex. These had been proposed by Freud, Jung, and others including Bleuler, the director of the hospital where she had been a patient. Apart from one theory suggesting that negative feelings arose from the closeness of the sexual organs to those for excretion, these explanations were mostly concerned with the social risks involved in sex – including attacks from rivals and fear of social exclusion. The explanation she quoted from Jung is interesting: he suggested that people's anxiety about sex might be linked to fears of future conflicts of interest with their own children: 'To be fruitful provokes one's downfall: at the rise of the next generation, the previous one has exceeded its peak. Our descendants become our most dangerous enemies for whom we are unprepared. They will survive and take power from our enfeebled hands.' The quotation from Jung was apposite, because Spielrein was about to draw attention to a similar conflict of interest between male and female.

Spielrein argued that most of these explanations were fine up to a point, but also incomplete. She emphasized that a feeling of anxiety was entirely normal and moved to the forefront of feelings as soon as 'the possibility of fulfillment of the wish first appears'. She then posed her opening question for a second time, with even more urgency: 'One feels the enemy inside oneself, in one's glowing love which forces one, with iron necessity, to do what one doesn't want to do: one feels the end, the fleetingness, from which one vainly tries to flee to distances unknown. "Is that all?" one wants to ask. "Is this the climax, and nothing beyond?" What happens to the individual in the sexual act that could justify such a mood?'

There can little doubt that Spielrein was describing her own sexual experiences with Jung. Her emphasis here on the negative side of sexual experience was to prove problematical. She seemed to have moved from talking about ambivalence, to something rather more extreme: let-down of a dramatic kind following orgasm. Although such an experience is well known, and has been described for centuries, it is obviously not the only possible outcome of sex. Her comments led people to wonder why she had talked about disappointment but not tenderness, and on the wish to flee but not commitment.

This key part of her paper now follows. In the published version the section is entitled 'Biological Facts'. These few short paragraphs contain the essence of Spielrein's argument. They are entirely unlike anything written by Freud, Jung, or other contemporary writers on sex like Krafft-Ebing or Havelock Ellis. Indeed, there appears to be nothing similar to them in the psychological literature for almost another century. They are worth reading carefully because the strengths and weaknesses of her theory rest on these paragraphs. (For readers who are unfamiliar with biological language, there is a simpler paraphrase of her theory at the end of the book).

'During reproduction, a union of female and male cells occurs. The unity of each cell thus is destroyed and, from the product of this destruction, new life originates. Following production of a new generation, many lower creatures e.g. the mayfly, forfeit their lives, dying off. Creation for this organism is undertaken for survival and is simultaneously destructive to the adult. The individual must strongly hunger for this new creation in order to place its own destruction in creation's service.'

'In more highly organized multicellular systems, the whole individual will obviously not be destroyed during the sexual act. However, the fewer number of germ cells [eggs or sperm] comprising the reproductive unit are not merely indifferent elements of the organism. They are intimately associated with the entire life of the individual. They contain, in a concentrated form, the generative power [genes] by which they have continually influenced the organism's and their own development. Fertilization destroys these important substances.'

'The fusion of germ cells during copulation mimics the correspondingly intimate union of two individuals: a union in which one forces its way into the other. The difference is merely quantitative: it is not the entire individual that is incorporated, but only a part of it that, at this instant, represents the essence of the entire organism. The male component merges with the female component that becomes reorganized and assumes a new form mediated by the unfamiliar intruder. An alteration comes over the whole organism: destruction and reconstruction, which under usual circumstances always accompany each other, occur rapidly. The organism discharges its sexual product as if it were one its excretions.'

'It would be highly unlikely if the individual did not at least surmise, through corresponding feelings, these internal deconstructive-reconstructive events. The joyful feeling of coming into being that is present within the reproductive drive is accompanied by a feeling of resistance, of anxiety or disgust. This does not arise from spatial proximity to the excreta or from the negativity of a renunciation of sexual activity; the feeling directly corresponds to the destructive component of the sexual instinct.'

What this passage mainly offers is a description of the biological events of sex. It describes how a man penetrates a woman and discharges sperm into her vagina. Fertilization takes place, and the egg then undergoes internal destruction and reconstitution in order to form an embryo. However, Spielrein clearly does more than offer an account of the 'biological facts' of sex. She draws attention to the way it involves some significant parallel processes. For example, just as the man physically invades the woman, so one of his sperm invades her egg. Similarly, just as the man and woman embrace, so the genetic material of egg and sperm combines rapidly. She also draws a parallel between these physical events of sex and the feelings that surround it. Seen through the eyes of modern biology, there are three specific elements in her argument that almost seem to jump off the page because of their originality and prescience. These elements are as follows:

1. 'The individual must strongly hunger for this new creation in order to place its own destruction in creation's service.' In other words, she points out that *reproduction predominates over survival* in evolution. Although we aren't mayflies, our fate is essentially the same as theirs: our offspring will outlive us, and our lives are oriented towards their survival rather than ours. This principle forms the basis of modern evolutionary theory: we devote our energy primarily not to keeping our own individual identity alive, but to transferring whatever we can to succeeding generations, either by direct or indirect means.

2. 'A union in which one forces its way into another'. Spielrein depicts *sex as a form of invasion, leading to the destruction of genes from both partners in the reconstitution of new life.* Modern biology too places an emphasis on sexual reproduction as a process in which each gender tries – sometimes with astonishing destructiveness – to impose its genetic will on the other, in order to prevail in the next generation.

3. 'It would be highly unlikely if the individual did not at least surmise, through corresponding feelings, these internal deconstructive-reconstructive events.' Spielrein's claim here is that,

at some level, *human feelings correspond with the biological facts of reproduction.* This claim frames emotions as something attuned to, and enacting, the processes of reproduction itself. This lies at the heart of a modern evolutionary understanding of emotions.

Implicitly in this section of her paper, and throughout her subsequent argument, she suggests that a *knowledge of these facts could be used as the basis for a new approach to the talking cure.* All these elements anticipate key ideas from many decades afterwards. Her initial question, and her three biological propositions point towards a modern evolutionary understanding of sexual psychology. Her overall approach to the talking cure prefigures the field known as evolutionary psychotherapy.

Nevertheless, it is important to note that Spielrein's conclusion itself is mistaken. The process of reproduction certainly includes destruction and reconstitution just as she describes, but it is incorrect to say that the reproductive *drive* itself contains a wish to destroy oneself – what she labelled a 'death instinct'. The purpose of sex is to create the next generation, and nothing else. Although both partners will eventually die, it makes no sense to describe this as an instinct, a drive, or a wish.

Similarly, Spielrein's notion that a drive towards destruction is the cause of ambivalence before sex or disappointment afterwards is unconvincing. A sense of psychological merger during sex is common, but there is no reason to imagine this relates in any way to what happens when a sperm merges with an egg. Spielrein's idea that we know intuitively during orgasm that we are losing our identity through the fusion of our sex cells is implausible.

For the moment, it is worth noting that her initial question is a worthwhile one, her argument contains some highly important propositions, but it would need quite a different formulation in order to make proper sense: I shall return to these propositions at the end of this book. But the most important thing to notice is that the foundations of her argument are not drawn from psychology alone, nor from philosophy, literature or mythology. They are biological.

SEVEN

Failure

Spielrein's audience in Vienna had difficulty in accepting what she said. This wasn't simply due to the overstatement in her introduction, or her puzzling conclusion. It was also because the rest of her presentation was so dense. Unlike the opening few pages, the main body of Spielrein's paper, where she expands on her argument, is complex and convoluted. Freud and Jung both commented on how difficult it was. Many modern readers have found it impenetrable. Spielrein fell prey to some of the typical failings of an academic novice. She tried to cover too much ground, and she showed off her erudition rather than staying close to her central argument. She also tried to show how her ideas were based on those of Freud and Jung, and how these could help to unite their two different approaches – something that neither man was ever going to appreciate. She dwelled a great deal on the notion that the pursuit of creation and joy are always accompanied by an instinct for sacrifice and self-immolation, and that the reproductive drive includes a destructive component. This theme dominates the rest of the paper.

After the 'biological facts', the next section of her paper, 'Individual Psychological Observations', is seventeen pages long in the published version. In it, she looks at the nature of the unconscious mind, dreams and symbolism. She examines how the basic conflict between creation and destruction is played out in different psychiatric conditions like hysteria and schizophrenia. Then there is a ten page section on 'Life and Death in Mythology' where she demonstrates how great writers and religious texts showed an intuitive understanding of this conflict, and of the connection between love and death. Her examples of this include Adam and Eve, Christ, and Siegfried in Wagner's 'Ring'.

Altogether in the published paper, she quotes Freud 25 times, Jung 11 times, and other significant psychoanalysts at least 25 times. She also refers again to her hospital psychiatrist Bleuler. She cites philosophers from Anaxagoras to Nietzsche and beyond. Her range of religious and literary references include the Bible, the Talmud, Maimonides, Gogol as well as a great deal of Wagner. It is without doubt a *tour de force*, but after the clarity of the opening section, much of it is confusing.

Yet through this dense forest of prose one can sometimes glimpse important biological principles. For example, in the section on individual psychology she challenges Freud for proposing that humans are governed by the pursuit of pleasure for its own sake. Spielrein disagrees, arguing that the pursuit of reproduction lies behind this and is even more important. 'Collective desires living within us', she argues, 'do not correspond to personal desires'.

She backs up her argument by looking at masochism, the sexual desire for pain: 'a wish for self-injury, a joy in pain, is…thoroughly incomprehensible' she wrote, 'if we believe merely in the existence of an ego that only desires pleasure'. Through analyzing her own masochism, Spielrein seems to have gained the confidence to put procreation over pleasure as a human drive. As we shall discover later, in modern biology the idea that the pursuit of reproductive success takes precedence over positive feeling is a key one. By contrast, Freud's principle that we seek pleasure for its own sake is regarded as entirely incorrect: sex has evolved to be pleasurable in order to promote procreation, not the other way around.

Summarizing her views on individual psychology, Spielrein points out: 'Self-preservation is a static drive because it must protect the existing individual from foreign influences; preservation of the species is a dynamic drive that strives for change, the resurrection of the individual in a new form. No change can take place without destruction of the former condition'.

John Kerr, in his classic account of the triangular relationship between Spielrein, Jung and Freud, fell short of understanding the strengths of her theory in terms of contemporary biology. However he was still able to sense something of the stature of her paper. 'In another age', Kerr remarked perceptively, 'it might have guaranteed her reputation.'

The lecture did not guarantee Spielrein's reputation: quite the contrary. It was a damp squib. We know quite a lot about what happened on the evening of Spielrein's lecture. The psychoanalyst Otto Rank took the minutes of the discussion and these are still extant – although they contain obvious inaccuracies. They suggest that many of the audience grabbed hold of the wrong end of the stick, and some grabbed the wrong stick altogether. Possibly Spielrein was nervous, and her delivery may have been tremulous or over-enthusiastic. We know that she concentrated on the denser, mythological section of her argument, which was the most confusing part. She probably could have made a clearer distinction between the evidence supporting her theory – from biology, psychology and mythology – and the main themes of the theory itself. Placing her main emphasis on intimations of mortality during intercourse and orgasm may have diminished any chances that her general biological approach would meet with acceptance.

However, not all the blame for the failure of the lecture can be placed at Spielrein's door. Rank, who took the notes, seems to have confused Spielrein's theory with the ideas of another Russian thinker, Ilya Mechnikov, who believed that people in later life had a benign anticipation of death and a readiness for it. In the discussion, many of those present used her talk as a pretext for promoting their own ideas or pursuing quarrels, sometimes on unrelated topics. Some attacked Spielrein's emphasis on philosophy, while others defended it. One person – Dr Stegmann, the only other woman in the Society – almost understood Spielrein: 'The fear of love is the fear of the death of one's own personality' she said, before lurching off into mysticism by adding: 'Love is indeed to be regarded as the transition from the small individual to the great cosmic life.' Some people mistakenly thought that Spielrein was presenting Jung's ideas, and they took the opportunity to have a go at him.

This was the line that Freud himself took at the beginning of his own response, as chairman. He used the occasion for his most explicit attack on Jung's approach to date. In what may have been a prepared speech, he offered a critique of Jung's recent mythological studies. The material of myths, he said 'has been transmitted to us in a state that does not permit us to make use of it for the solution of our problems. On the contrary, it must first be subjected to psychoanalytic elucidation'.

Having laid down the law in relation to myth, Freud then turned to biology, and directly to the heart of Spielrein's own argument. A psychological hypothesis, he asserted 'must be decided by way of individual psychological investigations. In contradistinction to our psychological point of view, however, the speaker attempted to base the theory of instincts on biological pre-suppositions (such as the preservation of the species)'. He could not have been clearer: psychoanalysis was completely separate from biology, and did not need to rest on biological principles. However, his remarks did at least pay Spielrein an indirect compliment: he implicitly acknowledged what she was trying to do – to square the circle between psychoanalysis and biology.

At the end of the evening, Spielrein apologized for not having made the biological fundamentals of her theory clearer at the start of her talk. For the sake of her theory, we might wish that she had made the biological theme far more prominent throughout the whole lecture, rather than concentrating so much on trying to reconcile Jung and Freud through making connections between dreams and myths. It might have provided additional evidence that she was on the kind of evolutionary track that her successors were to follow many decades later. However, given Freud's stated view, it is highly unlikely that it would have made a difference either way. As John Kerr comments: 'From the perspective of the young Fraulein Doktor, it must have been a terribly disappointing evening.'

EIGHT

The world of biology

There were many reasons why the lecture went down so badly. Incomprehension, in-fighting, sexism, and concern about Spielrein's sexuality no doubt all played a part. But the most important factor was hostility to biological thinking. To understand why this was so strong, we need to look more closely at the two worlds that she was trying to connect: biology and psychoanalysis. First of all we need to look at the position of biology in her time.

Spielrein had just completed her medical studies. She was doing so during a time of possibly the most dramatic revolution in scientific thinking in human history. She had been born only twenty five years after Darwin published 'The Origin of Species'. It was Darwin who established the principle that evolution happened through random variation from generation to generation: this led to 'natural selection' of the variations that best fitted the environment. Later, in 'The Descent of Man, he described how natural selection combined with 'sexual selection' of the organisms that were most effective in mating. Randomness in inheritance – the kind of destructive and reconstitutive processes that Spielrein described as part of reproduction – was essential to Darwinian thinking. It stood in contrast to so-called 'Lamarckian' ideas, which suggested that parents could hand down *acquired* knowledge directly through their genes.

One of Darwin's hopes was to develop a theory of psychology based on evolution. He published an entire book on 'The Expression of the Emotions in Man and Animals'. In it, he speculated on how far our unconscious reasons for certain emotions, such as childhood fears, were evolutionary in origin. He anticipated the day when 'psychology will be based on a new foundation, that of the necessary acquirement of each mental power and capacity by graduation.' Sadly, this hope for an evolutionary science of psychology wasn't realized. Darwin bequeathed his psychological papers to his friend George Romanes, who tried to develop them into a coherent theory of psychology but failed, largely because he fell prey to Lamarckian and similar fallacies. So did Darwin's other immediate successors in the field of psychology.

On the purely biological front, however, there were some stunning discoveries and it was these that formed the background for Spielrein's theory . Most of these were made in the German-speaking world. In 1876 a biologist called Oskar Hertwig first described seeing how a sperm penetrates an egg – the process described quite accurately by Spielrein as resembling the penetration that takes place during intercourse. (She may well have had a textbook illustration of Hertwig's discovery in her mind as she prepared her lecture.) Then, in 1893, August Weismann made the crucial distinction between so-called 'germ cells' that carry genetic information from generation to generation in the form of sperm and eggs, and the ordinary cells of the body, that carry out every other function but will all inevitably die.

Weismann is generally regarded as the greatest biologist of the nineteenth century after Darwin. He had begun his career as a committed Lamarckian, but ended up putting the last nail into the coffin of Lamarck's ideas. He showed how genes must be passed on from one generation to the next without any possibility of being affected by experiences which take place during the individual's lifetime. Weismann's discovery of the role of germ cells lay at the heart of Spielrein's theory. She understood that these cells governed development of everything in the human individual, including their own self-development as eggs and sperm. We might nowadays call this process 'genetic programming'. Weismann also made some fundamental discoveries concerning chromosomes. He worked out that fertilization of an egg by a sperm leads to a mixture of chromosomes from both parents in the resulting embryo, which also fits in with Spielrein's description.

A further surge of research into the biology of sex took place in the first decade of the twentieth century. People rediscovered the genetic experiments of Gregor Mendel, which confirmed and expanded on Darwin's ideas about inheritance. A Swiss contemporary of Spielrein, Johann Friedrich Miescher, identified a substance in chromosomes that he called 'nuclein' and we now recognize as DNA. An American, Thomas Hunt Morgan discovered that pairs of chromosomes embrace and exchange some material before they finally separate from each other to make a definitive egg or sperm. Two other American researchers discovered that eggs carry an extra X chromosome while sperm may carry either an X or a Y chromosome but not both. This means that fertilization may add a Y to the egg's X chromosome, leading to a male offspring, or it may add another X, so that the child is a girl.

In an outstanding medical school like the one in Zurich, there would have been an atmosphere of great excitement about such advances. Spielrein would undoubtedly have been aware of this research. Everything she wrote is consistent with it. As she clearly understood, all the discoveries of reproductive biology pointed in exactly the same direction. The genes we pass on to our children and our descendants are not of our choosing. In a profound sense they are no longer 'us'. They are a random collection of the genes that have been selected in the struggle for survival. It was an understanding of this process that enabled Spielrein to offer her own somber but correct account of the difference between each of us as individuals and our sexual bequests to posterity. The process of reproduction is inherently destructive and reconstitutive: of the egg or sperm as these formed within the individual, and then in the embryo they created jointly. The drive to reproduce is so powerful that it commits individuals to surrender their own genetic material to this destruction and reconstitution.

NINE

The world of psychoanalysis

If we now contrast the world of psychoanalysis at the beginning of the twentieth century to that of biology, we find a very different picture. The movement was very young. Its founder, Sigmund Freud, had only coined the word psychoanalysis in 1896 – barely seven years before Sabina entered the Burghölzli. It was outside the academic mainstream. To some it appeared scandalous. There was no doubt in anyone's mind that it was revolutionary. Freud had discovered an extraordinarily simple method for relieving mental distress: asking patients to lie down on a couch and speak of anything that came into their minds, including their sexual fantasies and their dreams. It was named 'the talking cure' not by Freud himself, but by a young woman called Bertha Pappenheim, who had hysterical symptoms similar to Spielrein. She was a patient of one of Freud's mentors, Joseph Breuer, who was the first person ever to try out this kind of method.

Alongside his method, Freud developed a set of powerful theories of how the mind functions. He described how the mind works at an unconscious level – at the level of hidden drives, desires and motivations. He put the sexual drive and its associated pleasure at the centre of everything, and he proposed that adult mental disturbance had its origins in unconscious sexual conflict. One of his most important ideas was the Oedipus complex: the proposition that every boy unconsciously aims to gain the sexual affection of his mother, and to destroy his father (or the other way round for girls).

A key claim that Freud made for all his theory was that it depended wholly on listening to the patient. Although he had a past career as a distinguished neurological doctor, he had put this behind him. The only way to examine the mind, he now believed, was to map it by means of the words and dreams of living people. In other words, he had gradually moved away from biology in the search for a pure science of psychology. This was the great strength of his theory. It also led to potential weakness. It meant that psychoanalytic theory was subjective. It derived entirely from one mind examining that of another, or indeed from one mind examining itself. Although Freud had originally drawn on many of the ideas of Charles Darwin and his successors, the whole discourse of psychoanalysis had broken loose from an anchorage in biology, and was now anchored in the authority of Freud himself.

'I try in general', he wrote 'to keep psychology clear from everything that is different in nature from it, even biological lines of thought'. The reasons for this are complex. Some still regard it as Freud's genius to propose that there might be a science that used as its sole material the study of the mind in the consulting room. Others can see the pragmatic and political advantages of his approach: a science that stood by itself stood to gain a higher status than one that was dependent on other sciences such as biology – or indeed on medicine. Freud was also keen for psychoanalysis to be opened up to lay practitioners. While continuing to come under attack from many of the leaders of mainstream medicine, psychoanalysis became highly successful as a social and cultural movement, as well as a school of psychology.

There was possibly another factor too. Freud might have once been a skilled biologist in the technical sense, when he carried out his early studies in neuro-anatomy and pathology, but he was never a great evolutionary theorist. Along with sexologists of the time like Krafft-Ebing and Havelock Ellis, he believed that some mental problems resembled – and perhaps even were – forms of regression to earlier evolutionary states. He took an explicitly Lamarckian stance in some of his writing: in other words, he argued that environmental pressures could bring about adaptations that could then be inherited. 'Lamarck's theory of evolution', he wrote, 'coincides with the final outcome of psychoanalytic thinking'. As time passed, he seems to have become out of touch with the evidence in biology that conclusively disproved these principles. It would have become hard for him to harmonize his psychological ideas with strict Darwinian principles of descent as Spielrein did.

While Freud continued to refer in rather general terms to the evolutionary origin of the human mind, he gave up any serious attempt to follow through this idea in a way that would have convinced any biologist of his time or since. Theoretically, as well as practically, it served his purposes to let biology slip into the background and then to disappear altogether. As a result, he effectively ensured that virtually all the different forms of the talking cure that emerged during the rest of the century – even those that explicitly rejected his theories – never considered a return to their biological roots for many decades afterwards.

This holds true for Jung too. Some Jungians have argued that Jung was more in tune with evolutionary thinking than Freud. This is because Jung traced the workings of the human mind to enduring patterns of ideas, images and expectations – so-called 'archetypes' – that had been laid down in ancient collective experience rather than the more recent influences of infancy and childhood. There is some substance in this claim. However, Jung's frequent references to tendencies that we inherit as a species are rather vague, and they are distinctly thin in terms of biological reasoning. They make it clear that he too took a Lamarckian view of the matter. He mistakenly imagined that cultures, races and social groups could rapidly acquire archetypal tendencies that would then be passed on through inheritance.

This, among other things, may account for some of Jung's less palatable racial beliefs, including his anti-semitism. There is no suggestion anywhere in his writings that he tried to understand the collective unconscious in terms of natural selection and sexual selection, as opposed to an outmoded belief in the possibility of passing on acquired knowledge to one's descendants.

When Spielrein joined the Vienna Psychoanalytic Society in 1911, she did so at a moment of immense crisis in its existence. In the previous month, Freud had expelled the followers of Alfred Adler, for placing too much emphasis on biology in the role of mental illness. The very day before Spielrein's lecture, her mentor Eugen Bleuler had himself resigned from the Society, protesting that dogmas and expulsions were more appropriate for a cult or political party than a science. Freud was now placing his hopes in Bleuler's student, Jung, as a loyal ally and successor.

As a Swiss Christian psychiatrist, with a growing reputation of his own, Jung seemed the perfect person to help psychoanalysis break out from the world of Viennese Jews. At the same time, it was already clear that his interest in mythology might lead to another split in the movement. The evening of 29 November 1911 was in many ways a turning point for the entire movement of psychoanalysis. It was the moment when Freud defined what psychoanalysis must be and – more important – what it absolutely must *not* be.

One of the 'must nots' was Jung's mythology, and the other was Spielrein's biology. It was absolutely not permissible for psychoanalysis to be a *deductive* method, setting out from the established principles of evolution. Instead it must be purely *inductive*, based on what patients said in the presence of their analysts. As he said on the night of Spielrein's lecture, the former were mere 'pre-suppositions'. These were no alternative, in his view, to 'individual psychological investigations'.

Spielrein's theory was an immediate and explicit challenge to both Freud and Jung. It went beyond Freud's concern about what happens in childhood, or what adults describe as happening to them in the past. It went beyond Jung's concern with how human beings collectively fashion the images and myths that then govern their behaviour. Instead, Spielrein posed the question: what underlies these? Her answer was clear: we must look to biology to make sense of these. This placed psychological thinking in a biological perspective in a way that neither Freud nor Jung ever achieved. It also meant neither man could accept any part of her argument whatsoever.

TEN

Aftermath

After her lecture, Spielrein stayed in Vienna for another six months. During that time she prepared her paper for publication and continued to attend meetings of the Vienna Psychoanalytic Society. Meanwhile, the sparring between Jung and Freud continued, with Spielrein's theory often getting caught in the middle. The correspondence between the three of them during this period is, if anything, even more disturbing than the letters they exchanged three years previously about her entanglement with Jung. We can sense how Spielrein the woman and Spielrein the biological theorist became conflated in the minds of the two men, as they battled against her – and against each other.

The day after Spielrein gave her lecture, Freud wrote to Jung about what she had said. He admitted cheerfully that he regarded her as a spokeswoman for her mentor. 'Fräulein Spielrein read a chapter from her paper yesterday (I almost wrote 'your' paper!) and it was followed by an illuminating discussion. I have hit on a few objections to your (this time I mean it) method of dealing with mythology. I brought them up in the discussion with the little girl.' Having sent this shot across Jung's bows, he backed away from confrontation, with a laddish wink concerning Jung's fling with his young patient: 'I must say she is rather nice and I am beginning to understand.' He then rounded off with an attack on her biological approach, making it clear that this was no better than a mythological one: 'What troubles me most is that Fräulein Spielrein wants to subordinate the psychological material to biological considerations; this dependency is no more acceptable than a dependency on philosophy, physiology or brain anatomy. *Psychoanalysis goes by itself.*'

Jung no doubt disagreed on the topic of mythology, but he was more than happy to endorse Freud's other point: 'I know, of course, that Spielrein operates too much with biology', he wrote to

Freud. 'But she didn't learn that from me, it is home-grown'. Jung's statement here seems to be entirely truthful. Spielrein's diaries and the correspondence between them confirm that she developed the theory alone, and any discussion of it with Jung was always initiated by her.

Early in 1912, Spielrein submitted 'Destruction As The Cause of Coming Into Being' for publication in the Yearbook of the psychoanalytic movement. She sent it to Jung as the editor. She described it as 'the product of our love, the project which is our little son Siegfried'. After the failure of her lecture she feared it would be rejected. 'This study means more to me than my whole life,' she told him, 'and that is why I am so fearful'. He sent an acknowledgment of receipt, but it was so formal and cold that she considered suicide by hanging herself. She wrote in her diary: 'I thought of how lovingly my mother used to wrap a scarf around my neck to keep me from catching cold, how she raised me to this point, and then…her only daughter…because of a…Oh, because of a man who has smashed my whole life.'

Eventually, Jung had a look at Spielrein's paper. Even though it was now almost a year since she had sent him the original draft of her lecture, this was probably the first time he had actually read her theory. He did not like what he saw. He wrote to Freud and described it using a Latin quotation from Horace: 'What at the top is a lovely woman ends below in a fish'. The comment has obscene undertones. It is also impossible to avoid noting that he displays exactly the kind of ambivalent attitude to female genitals – simultaneous lust and disgust – that exactly fits Spielrein's description of sexual ambivalence in her paper. Knowing of his intimate contact with Spielrein's body, it is hard not to be shocked by his disloyalty, and his unashamed expression of physical recoil from her.

Jung and Freud voiced another concern to each other: her ideas could not be trusted, because she herself was so troubled sexually. 'She seems abnormally ambivalent', Freud wrote. 'Her paper is heavily weighted with her own complexes', Jung suggested. Both men no doubt realised that Spielrein's mention of 'my involvement with sexual problems' at the beginning of her paper referred to her personal problems as much as her clinical experience. Whatever reservations they may have had about her explanation for sexual anxiety, they may also have been worried that her vivid description of the emotional deflation following orgasm was a veiled attack on her former lover. The two men knew a great deal about each other's sexual relationships and disappointments, so that any judgments concerning Spielrein's 'ambivalence' can hardly be considered objective. It would certainly have suited both men to agree about her own failings rather than to dwell on their own.

The most telling exchange in the correspondence during this period is one between Jung and Spielrein. In March 1912 Jung wrote to her as follows: 'As I read your paper I found uncanny parallels with my own new work appearing in it which I did not at all suspect, for until then I had always read your title incorrectly: '*distinction*' instead of 'destruction' and was puzzled about it…Your destruction wish is certainly correct. We desire not only the ascent but also the descent and the end.'

Distinction instead of destruction? How was it possible for anyone, let alone Jung, to read even the first page of her paper and fail to see it was about destruction and creation? Besides, we know she had been talking with him about her theory for six years. To her it was their 'Siegfried', the progeny of their intellectual and emotional partnership, the substitute for the son they never had. She had described it as 'more than my whole life'. How would Spielrein have reacted to his mis-reading, and the casual way he mentioned it? Her reply to this letter no longer exists, but John Kerr speculates that she 'exploded'.

Jung's reply certainly seems to confirm this supposition. Again he appeased her, while planting the blame for any misunderstanding squarely on her: 'My Dear, You are upsetting yourself quite unnecessarily again. When I said there were "uncanny" similarities, you took that again much too literally. I was intending it much more as a compliment to you. Your study was extraordinarily intelligent and contains splendid ideas whose priority I am happy to acknowledge as yours. The death tendency or death wish was clear to you before it was to me, understandably!'

Reading these letters, it is hard to avoid the impression that Jung had never really listened to Spielrein when she talked to him about her theory. In spite of his claims to find 'uncanny parallels' with his own work, there is no evidence here or anywhere else that he understood the theory, in which neither the term 'death tendency' or 'death wish' ever occurred.

There is one more telling exchange in the correspondence. Freud had maintained a dignified silence concerning Jung's quotation about a woman 'ending below in a fish.' But later on, he let Jung know that Spielrein had visited him to say she was leaving Vienna: 'Spielrein, to whom I was glad not to mention your criticism, came to say good-bye a few days ago and discussed certain intimate matters with me.'

We will never know what these 'intimate matters' were. Possibly some of them related to Jung. It is hard to think of any other reason why Freud should have referred to them in his letter. But it was the last time Spielrein's name appeared in their correspondence. A few months later they were no longer on speaking terms. We can only speculate about the part played by 'intimate matters' in leading Freud to make his final decision about Jung, and to dissociate himself from the man he had appointed not so long before as his 'son and heir'.

The following year he wrote to Spielrein: 'My personal relationship with your Germanic hero has definitely been shattered. His behaviour was too bad. Since I received the first letter from you, my opinion of him has greatly altered,' Later the same year he wrote: 'I imagine that you love Dr J so deeply because you have not brought to light the hatred he merits. When I had to take sides at the beginning of our correspondence, it looked as if it would work out. I am glad that I am now as little responsible for his personal achievements as I am for his scientific ones.'

ELEVEN

Experience and theory

Much of Freud and Jung's criticism of Spielrein's theory was based on their reservations about her as a person, and their knowledge of her personal experiences. In effect, she was claiming the right to use her own limited and untypical repertoire of sexual experiences as a source of new psychological theory.

This raises a fundamental question about personal conflict as a source of insight. Much of Freud's own theory had arisen in the first place from an analysis of his own inner conflicts. Many of his followers, like Jung, had analyzed themselves in order to construct their own theories. Other analysts had then been patients of Freud, or of each other. Several had subsequently been each others' lovers as well. In the early days, they all openly acknowledged that conflicts could be a source of discovery as well as discomfort. At times, members of the society offered theories that were valued precisely because everyone knew that these had arisen from their own psychological problems or the relationships they had had with each other. Yet at other times, their ideas were rejected for exactly the same reason.

As a result, Freud and his followers were inclined to use one kind of argument when it suited them, and the other kind when it did not. Instead of evaluating a new idea from a colleague on its own merits, they tended to accept it when it fitted their own existing theories, reject it when it did not, and then praise or attack the personality of the colleague accordingly. In the case of Spielrein, it is clear that she had drawn on her own troubled imagination to work out her theory of sex and destruction. But in doing so, she put herself at risk of being doubly dismissed. If people did not like her ideas, they could undermine these by blaming them on her mental state. Ultimately, this is the position that both Jung and Freud took.

It is likely – indeed almost certain – that Spielrein's own masochistic desires and fantasies are what led her to formulate the question that led her towards her theory. However, the question that neither man addressed was whether any psychoanalytic theory could ever stand in its own right without being called into question on account of its proponent's human weaknesses. Spielrein had been the victim of their inability to separate person from theory, and of their deflected contempt for each other.

There is an irony in the way Jung and Freud dismissed Spielrein's ideas. When they finally fell out, they used exactly the same tactic to criticize each other as they had when rejecting Spielrein's views. In one of his final letters to Jung, Freud offered this personal gibe: 'It is a convention among us analysts that none of us need feel ashamed of his own bit of neurosis. But one who while behaving abnormally keeps shouting that he is normal gives grounds for suspicion that he lacks insight into his illness. Accordingly, I propose that we abandon our personal relations entirely'. Jung replied with a suggestion that Freud should look into his own psyche for the cause of the rift, signing off with a Shakespearean flourish: 'I accede to your wish that we abandon our personal relations, for I never thrust my friendship on anyone. You yourself are the best judge of what this moment means to you. "The rest is silence".'

There was one further irony to the story. Jung did in time borrow Spielrein's idea as she had feared, but published it in a form that no-one could really follow. Freud, too, eventually took it up and made something different out of it as well. Appalled by the destructiveness of the First World War, he wrote a book in 1920 called 'Beyond the Pleasure Principle'. In it, he proposed the idea of a 'death instinct', or the drive to bring about one's own extinction. In one of his few published references to her, he acknowledged Spielrein's influence in formulating the idea, while confessing that he did not really understand her own reasoning when she originally proposed it. But typically for Freud, he did not relate the death instinct directly to biology or to procreation as Spielrein had done. Instead, he saw it as something that existed for its own sake. He likened it to the law of entropy, whereby the energy of any physical system declines over time to zero.

Freud's version of the death instinct – a destructive counterpart to the creative drive of sex – has remained an important idea for some psychoanalysts. They have contrasted Freud's version with Spielrein's. They have criticised hers as pathological, since she saw sex and death as inextricably intertwined rather than standing in opposition to each other. They continue to draw the conclusion that her own sexual problems led her to propose such a view. They may be right, but it is not clear why this should disqualify all the other elements of her theory. Her conclusions may have been erroneous, but her premises were not.

From a twenty-first century perspective, Spielrein's biological approach does not seem an extraordinary one to have taken. Indeed, it seems entirely logical. Why should one want to limit the search for the causes of mental functioning, and mental distress, to childhood, or culture, or indeed to any such arbitrary point? As Spielrein tried to show, there was no inherent contradiction between her view and those of both Freud and Jung. It was possible to take an biological perspective that would at the same time encompass the mental processes of adults, the experiences and fantasies of childhood, and the productions of art and culture. Sadly, such a view was not acceptable to either man. If there was ever any uncertainty about this in the early days, it had ceased with the expulsion of Adler and the resignation of Bleuler – both proponents of a biological approach – at exactly the time that Spielrein appeared on the scene. And as the quarrels intensified between Freud and Jung, neither of them had been in the mood to listen to a twenty-six year old female peacemaker.

TWELVE

Departure

We can now move on to the next stage in Spielrein's own story, and consider how she developed her ideas in the years following 1911. After she had given her lecture, we know that she stayed in Vienna for only a few more months. During that time, she took an active part in the Vienna Psychoanalytic Society. She saw some patients that Freud had sent her. In the winter she visited Rostov-on-Don. In the following summer she got married.

The marriage seems to have come out of the blue. In February 1912, on the day she had contemplated suicide, she recorded in her diary that she had a dream that she would soon marry. A colleague had also read her palm and predicted that her fate would take a new turn. A few months afterwards, her diary includes this sentence: 'On 14th June I married Dr Paul Scheftel. To be continued.' Extraordinarily, without any further comment, she reports another dream she has had. There is no further reference to him in her diary, nor in any of her own surviving letters.

Paul Scheftel was a Russian Jew like herself, and a medical doctor. Possibly her parents introduced him when she was in Rostov. It is also possible that the marriage was more of an agreed arrangement, than a result of passion. If so, Spielrein was following an established family pattern: as we know, both her mother and her mother's father had been forced to give up relationships with Christians, before settling down into conventional Jewish marriages. She had also written of her intention to find a man who resembled Jung, and whom she might learn to love in time. Perhaps Dr Scheftel fitted that description. Her marriage may have been an attempt to exorcise this.

A letter from Freud congratulating her on the occasion suggests as much: 'So you are a married woman now. And as far as I am concerned that means you are half cured of your neurotic dependence on Jung. Otherwise you would not have decided to get married. The other half still remains; the question is what is to be done about that. My wish is for you to be cured completely…We had agreed that you would let me know before 1 Oct. whether you still intend to drive out the tyrant by psychoanalysis with me. Today I would like to put in a word or two about that decision. I imagine the man of whom you say so many nice things has rights as well…Let him first try to see how far he can tie you to himself and make you forget the old dreams…Meanwhile it might happen that someone else will turn up who will have more rights than both the old and new man put together.'

After her marriage, Spielrein moved from Vienna to Berlin. Later correspondence shows that her longing for Jung continued for at least another two years. The 'someone else' that Freud predicted did indeed turn up: in December 1913 she gave birth to her first daughter, Irma Renata. The child almost died at birth but mercifully recovered. Freud was pleased that the baby was female, and congratulated her. He hoped this would make it easier for her to give up the fantasy of having 'a blond Siegfried' with Jung. Around the outbreak of the First World War the following year, Spielrein moved from Berlin to Geneva, possibly because life in Germany at that time would not have been easy for a Russian.

Even in a neutral country, the war years were still not easy for her. For at least some of this time, she was without her husband. She worked for a while as a surgeon. 'I renounced any aspiration to personal creativity' she wrote to Jung, 'and simply fixed my sights on becoming a competent worker.' To her surprise, however, her creativity burst forth in an entirely new direction: musical composition.

We know about this period of her life only from her correspondence. She exchanged letters with Jung until 1919 and with Freud until 1923. There are gaps even here. Most of her letters to Freud have vanished, although his responses still exist. The tone of the letters from the two men is different. Freud's are mostly brief, avuncular and affectionate. One theme of her letters to Freud, however, was the difficulty of finding psychoanalytic work. On occasion, she wrote to him accusing him of not sending patients to her. He reproved her, saying there were none to send, and pointing out that both Adler and Jung had made the same accusation as a prelude to their schism with him. Later, she also asked Jung to help her find patients, even pleading with him: 'Where am I to find patients? Would you recommend me if I came to Zurich?'.

Jung as a rule wrote back at greater length than Freud but he veered between different moods, sometimes expansive but sometimes patronizing. Occasionally there was an anti-semitic flavor: 'There is a part of the Jewish soul which you are not yet living, because you still have your eye too much on the outside. That is, "unfortunately", the curse of the Jew…he is the murderer of his own prophets, even the Messiah.' He also expresses suspicion of women: 'My mistrust is aroused by the fickleness of the female spirit and its vain and tyrannical presumption.'

Spielrein wrote back to him without reproach, careful to clarify her own ideas, diligent in inviting his. As John Kerr points out: 'It should be noted that while they are quite difficult for the modern reader, they represent an honest and intelligent effort to come to grips with the theories of Jung, Adler and Freud. Beyond itemizing the differences, Spielrein also tried to forge a synthesis among the three, using as her point of departure the theory she had herself outlined in 1912.' In some letters, she returned to the themes of her Vienna lecture, making an explicit link with Darwin's ideas. 'Natural history', she explained in one letter to Jung , 'recognizes only two drives, the drive for self-preservation and the drive for preservation of the species.'

She even raised the question of whether there is in fact only one drive – the drive for reproduction – so that the drive for survival is always subservient to this. This is the most modern formulation that she ever offered of the relationship between sex and survival: it is the one that evolutionary biologists now regard as conclusive.

In her letter, she follows up another theme from her paper, by speculating that infant development is a preparation for later sexual maturity: 'To express my own opinion, I would include the instinct for self-preservation in the instinct for preservation of the species. The need to survive merges imperceptibly with the need to die and be reborn. In its initial stages the instinct for preservation completely coincides with the instinct for preservation of the species, although with very tiny creatures one cannot yet determine whether they love the mother's breast, for example, because…one loves the breast "physically" for itself or, what I think most likely, because it satisfies the need for hunger and in addition provides warmth and peace, and for this reason the physical contact becomes pleasurable, which is already the beginning of sexual feeling.'

Again, she is here partly anticipating ideas that were to play a part in evolutionary thinking a century later: all development is directed towards eventual reproduction. But in an earlier letter, Jung had already let her know his view of such an idea: 'It is inadmissible. We cannot allow a psychology based on biology to cut the throat of a psychology of the ego'. As we saw with Freud's claim that 'psychoanalysis goes by itself', there is no logical argument offered to back up this bald assertion.

Later that year, in another letter, Spielrein notes: 'it is very instructive for me that you and Freud accuse each other of the same thing, that is, of applying biological assumptions to psychology. And yet neither of you interprets instinct as something biological. Freud studies chiefly the psychological manifestations of an "instinct" ie feelings of pleasure or displeasure which give rise to corresponding wishes. He assumes sensations of pleasure and displeasure as the source of all psychic occurrences in us. According to him, we all strive for the pleasurable and suppress everything which is unpleasurable…' She was thoroughly aware, it appears, that her approach made sense biologically and theirs did not.

She also tried persistently to heal the rift between the two men. 'You should have the courage to recognize Freud in all his grandeur' she wrote to Jung in 1918,' even if you do not agree with him on every point, even if in the process you might have to credit Freud with many of your own accomplishments.' He remained impervious to these proposals, as did Freud, who wrote to a colleague about Jung: 'His bad theories do not compensate me for his disagreeable character'. He had already confided in Spielrein that he had given up on his search for a non-Jewish successor altogether. 'I am, as you know, cured of my last shred of predilection for the Aryan cause.'

Finally, in one of Jung's last recorded letters to her, there is an apology of sorts for his past behaviour, and a confession of how central she was to his own emotional and intellectual development: 'The love of S. for J. made the latter aware of something he had previously only vaguely suspected, namely of a power in the unconscious that shapes our destiny, a power that later led him to things of the greatest importance. The relationship had to be "sublimated" because otherwise it would have led to delusion and madness…Sometimes we must be unworthy in order to live'.

THIRTEEN

Independence

During the war, Spielrein had developed an interest in another area of psychology: the origin and development of children's speech. After the war finished, she gave a lecture on this in the Hague. Later the lecture was published in a revised form. Once again, Spielrein's thinking was far in advance of its time. She anticipated ideas that became central in the field of child psychology during the coming century: the social nature of infants, the importance of child observation in understanding the human mind, and issues concerning attachment, separation and loss. Yet the paper is totally unlike the lecture she had once given in Vienna. Her argument is focussed. Her voice is now strong, independent and utterly lucid. There are a few references to Freud but none to Jung. It is clear that she is now her own woman.

A quotation from the summary at the end of the paper gives an indication of the richness and clarity of Spielrein's thought, and of her foresight: 'The word "Mama" (in baby pronunciation "mö-mö-mö") reproduces the act of suckling. The word Papa (=pö-pö) stems from the phase when the satisfied infant is playing with the breast. Both words owe their origin to suckling. Like no other, the act of suckling is fundamental to the most important experiences of the child's life: here it gets to know the bliss of having its hunger stilled, but it learns too that this bliss has an end and has to be won all over again. The infant experiences for the first time the fact that there is a world outside itself; its contact with the mother's body plays a part in this by offering some resistance to the movements of the infant's mouth. And finally the infant learns that there is a refuge in this external world which is desirable not only because there its hunger is satisfied, but because it is warm and soft and protected from all dangers. If we have once in our lives felt "Let this moment last for ever, it is so beautiful" it was surely at this time. Here the child learns for the first time to love, in the widest sense of the word, that is to experience contact with another person, independently of feeling, as the highest bliss.'

Spielrein's fascination with child psychology was triggered by her own experience as a mother. She was explicit about this in her writing, and sometimes referred directly to her daughter Renata's early speech and behaviour. But there was clearly also a strong if unspoken link with her fascination with biology and evolution. In turning from the nature of sexual reproduction to the world of the infant, Spielrein was certainly aware of the connections between the two. She would also have known that she was following an important biological tradition: seeking clues to the bigger picture in the details of the smaller one.

The adjustment in her focus may also tell us something about her own personality. Unlike Freud and Jung, she was neither a politician nor an evangelist. She may have understood that her theory offered a way of linking the inner and outer worlds, and the world of psychoanalysis with the world of medicine. But she had also discovered that there was no point in preaching such a message from the mountain tops to skeptical and sectarian colleagues. For now, she chose to labour in the foothills. Maybe she hoped that her small discoveries might one day help to promote her bigger theory. We cannot know.

Ironically, everything Spielrein described about child development is more or less taken for granted by child psychologists nowadays. Such ideas are nearly always ascribed to later researchers, especially Melanie Klein and Anna Freud. It is notable that Klein herself attended Spielrein's lecture in the Hague, which pre-dated her own writings on the infant's experience of its mother's breast. Unfortunately, the powerful reputations of these two women have eclipsed Spielrein's. In an essay on Spielrein, Sabine Richerbächer offers the following explanation: 'Spielrein was an independent person and someone with a will of her own who would not allow herself to be slotted into the interests of the psychoanalytic movement as a mere apparatchik. In the patriarchal structures of psychoanalysis she caused offence again and again...Thus we are faced with the strange finding that, of all disciplines, psycho-analysis, which is founded on a belief in the healing power of memory, stubbornly resists its own history'.

In yet another irony, a dispute over psychoanalytic theory between Melanie Klein and Anna Freud was later to cause the biggest schism since Jung and Freud broke up, and to lead to the exasperated departure of independently minded thinkers like the English psychiatrist Charles Rycroft, whose accusations of cultism echoed Eugen Bleuler's complaints fifty years before.

It is impossible to know how much Spielrein used her biological ideas to help her child or adult patients. There are some references in her writing to matters that she discussed with them. These suggest that she was caring and conscientious in attending to their symptoms and their stories. However, they give no hint of anything out of the ordinary, in terms of the ideas or interpretations she proposed to them. If her original thinking from the heady times in Zurich and Vienna influenced her clinical practice at all, it may only have been as a quiet meditation in the back of her mind. Or perhaps the underlying argument was no longer important to her. As many therapists have reported, once a theory has been formed and assimilated, it is possible to work with patients using acquired wisdom, experience and intuition alone, and setting the abstract ideas to one side.

We know in some detail about one of Spielrein's patients, because he was famous and he spoke about her. He was Jean Piaget, who later became one of the world's leading developmental psychologists. The two met up in 1920 when Spielrein moved to work in Geneva. They worked together at the Jean-Jacques Rousseau Institute there. She offered Piaget a 'didactic analysis', in other words an analysis that would help him understand himself and the method of treatment at the same time. (Nowadays treatment and training would be kept strictly separate, but this was not so at that time.) He visited her every morning at eight o'clock for eight months.

Piaget had mixed feelings about the experience. Disappointingly, he never cast much light on what it was like to be on the couch in Spielrein's consulting room. He claimed to have found it 'marvelous' to discover his own complexes, but he was also 'impervious to the theory.' He and Spielrein continued as colleagues and friends for some time afterwards, while going different ways professionally. Piaget remained in the realm of objective observations. Spielrein preferred to combine these with a sensitivity to subjective meaning as well.

Spielrein stayed in Geneva until 1923. She gave lectures on psychoanalysis, did some clinical work and supervision, and wrote theatre reviews for the *Journal de Genève*. She carried out research at the Psychological Institute under Freud's disciple and translator, Edouard Claparède. While there, she must have deposited her letters and diaries in the archives – or perhaps someone did this later on her behalf. The papers remained there unread for over fifty years. It was only their discovery in 1977 that led to a widespread realization of the importance of her relationships with Jung and Freud, and the role she played both in their friendship and their enmity. We can only speculate on her reasons for leaving her papers where she did. She was about to return to Russia, so it is possible she wanted to leave such important documents in a safer country. We should be grateful that she did so, as it is impossible to imagine that they might have survived if she had taken them with her back to Russia.

As for the reasons for going back to her native country, these too are a matter for speculation. Her decision may have been for financial reasons, for family ones, or – most probably – through an idealistic wish to promote psychoanalysis in Russia. She let Freud know that she was finally going home after nearly twenty years in the west. His reply is the last surviving letter to her from Freud:

'Dear Frau Doktor, I am in receipt of your letter and really believe you are right. Your plan to go to Russia seems to me much better than my advice to try out Berlin. In Moscow you will be able to accomplish important work...Lastly, you will be on home ground. These are difficult times for us all. I hope to hear from you soon, but would earnestly request that you write your address on the inside of your letter, which so few women are wont to do. Cordially yours, Freud.'

FOURTEEN

Back in Russia

Following the revolution of 1917, the Spielrein family had been dispossessed of their money, their possessions and their home in Rostov-on-Don. In 1920 her mother died. Her father was still alive and now working to combat illiteracy among workers. Her brothers Jan and Isaac had returned to Russia after completing their education in the west. Her remaining brother Emil had been there all along. Spielrein's husband was back in Rostov by now, practicing medicine, although he was living with another woman with whom he had a child.

After the civil war, it finally looked as if psychoanalysis might flourish in a reconstructed Russia. From 1922 Freud's works and the writings of some of his followers were published in Moscow. When completing a questionnaire in September 1923, applying for permission to settle in Moscow, she added two unconventional footnotes about her work:

'1. In a psychoanalytical institute it would be considered essential to have the children under personal observation, so that talks with the supervisors do not lead to a purely theoretical discussion and 'platonic' advice given 'in absentia'.

'2. I enjoy my work, and feel as if it were made for me, as if I were called to the work, and without it I see no other meaning to my life.'

Once in Moscow, Spielrein began work on a training programme for future analysts. Her seminar on child analysis attracted more participants than any of her colleagues'. Within a short time she was director of the child psychology department of the First Moscow University, and a scientific contributor at the State Psychoanalytic Institute . The Institute was at the forefront of thinking in its time. Two of Russia's greatest psychologists – Alexander Luria and Lev Vygotsky – collaborated with it, and may well have been influenced by Spielrein. As John Kerr points out: 'Listing the ten greatest psychologists of this century is a matter of fashion and taste but on anyone's list five names would inevitably appear and Spielrein knew all of them first hand: Freud, Jung, Piaget, Luria and Vygotsky.'

However, the honeymoon period for psychoanalysis in Russia did not last long. In 1925 the Institute was abolished on political grounds. Spielrein returned to her home town in the south of the country. She and her husband were reunited. In 1926 she gave birth to a second daughter, Eva, named after Spielrein's mother. She stayed at home for a while with her new baby, but then returned to work, partly in a psychiatric hospital and partly in a school. She also did some private practice. Now in her forties, Spielrein evidently gave the impression of quite a strange, unpractical and old-fashioned woman. She kept a large library of French and German books, but it seems that did not speak of her past in the west. In 1930 the Russian Psychoanalytical Society was also abolished, but she continued her work so far as was possible, sending one last paper on children's drawings to the leading psychoanalytic journal of the time, 'Imago', in 1933.

Writing in German, Russian or French, Spielrein published over thirty papers in the course of her career, many of them concerning child development. When her paper on speech development from 1923 was finally translated into English eighty years afterwards, her translator wrote as follows: 'Spielrein's paper conveys an impression of a richly creative and profoundly sensitive and insightful mind. It is a great loss that her work and thinking in the area of early developmental processes were not further elaborated and more widely known and appreciated at the time. She has indeed been sadly neglected.'

Adeline van Waning, a Dutch psychoanalyst who has written one of the most sympathetic reviews of Spielrein's professional writing, offered a similar view: 'Spielrein developed new ideas in the fields of the life of the instinct, child development and child analysis and the female psyche', she wrote. She was also creative in devising research set-ups. The themes of love, destruction and creativity are woven into her work and her life. The diversity in the partners she chose to work with – Jung, Freud, Piaget and – later in her life, her great linguistic and neurophysiological interests indeed show her to be a versatile and self-willed pioneer. So far, Sabina Spielrein has not received the attention she deserves.' The historian Sabine Richebächer has gone further. 'We have to ask ourselves', she writes, 'what forces are at work here to cut off psychoanalysis from remembering and recording historically the myths of its origins?'

As the nineteen-thirties progressed, it became increasingly precarious and indeed life-threatening to be a psychoanalyst in the Soviet Union. It was scarcely safer being a teacher, and in 1932 the journal 'The Teaching Profession' was abolished in its turn. In 1936 a pogrom started against any teachers who were deemed to be anti-communist.

Spielrein may still have been seeing some patients. She had a consulting room in the middle of the house, with a door but no windows. One psychoanalyst has argued that this suggests a wish to provide a womb-like environment in which her patients could 'experience the loss of ego that she sought herself'. A commentator with more imagination might consider other reasons why a woman pursuing a proscribed activity in a police state should have worked in this way. Unfortunately, such facile interpretations are quite common in psychoanalytic writing about Spielrein.

The life of the Spielrein family became hellish, along with the lives of so many of their contemporaries. In 1935 the secret police arrested her brother Isaac, a professor of physiology, for anti-Soviet propaganda He was sent to a corrective labour camp for five years. While there he was charged with spying on behalf of Germany, and shot the same day. Her two other brothers Jan and Emil – one a physicist and member of the USSR Academy of Sciences, and the other a senior lecturer in biology – followed him into the labour camps. Neither were heard of again. Their father, Nikolai Spielrein, was tortured. He died in 1938. Spielrein's husband Paul had died the previous year, and she approached his mistress with a proposal to share responsibility for all three daughters. They agreed that if one of them were to disappear, the other would take care of the girls.

The end came not at the hand of the Soviet secret police, but with the arrival of the Nazis. When the Second World War broke out in 1939, Russia had initially sided with Germany. Stalin and Hitler had agreed to collaborate in the destruction of Poland by invading it from the east and west respectively. The destruction of Europe's Jews had begun alongside this. As the Germans entered each Polish town and village, murder squads massacred all the Jewish men, women and children there, often burying them in pits, with or without shooting them first. But in 1941, Hitler turned against the Soviet Union as well. His armies and murder squads began to move together across eastern Poland and into Russia. Spielrein's daughter Renata, who was studying music in Moscow, moved back to be with her mother in Rostov. The German army reached there in November 1941. The Russian army managed to reclaim the city, although many of Rostov's population died during the ground fighting and in horrifying air raids. On 27 July 1942 the Germans took Rostov again, this time conclusively.

The most reliable account of Sabina Spielrein's death comes from the Russian psychoanalyst and historian Victor Ovcharenko: 'The last time she was seen was in the summer of 1942 in a column of Jews, destined for annihilation, whom the Nazis were driving on in the direction of the Zmeyevsky gully – an enormous ravine on the edge of the city, in which mass executions of peaceful citizens took place. Poorly dressed, mortally tired and occupied with thoughts only known to herself, Sabina Spielrein shuffled along the column together with her daughters. She and her daughters found their last refuge that day in the spilt blood of tens of thousands of corpses piled up in the Zmeyevsky gully. Thus drew to a close the dreadful symmetry of fate of the Spielrein family: the Communists shot three innocent people, and the National Socialists also shot three innocents.'

Sabina Spielrein was not only an innocent, in many senses of the word. She was a far-sighted thinker about human evolution and its implications. She was killed by men in the grip of a racist ideology that perverted evolutionary thinking to the point of madness. Incapable of understanding human destructiveness, they enacted it.

When she had been a patient in the Burghölzli nearly forty years earlier, Sabina Spielrein had written a fanciful 'Last Will' She declared that she wanted her body cremated: 'But no-one is to be present for this. Divide the ashes into three parts. Place one part in an urn and send it home. Scatter the second part on the ground over our biggest field. Plant an oak tree there and write on it: "I too was once a human being. My name was Sabina Spielrein". My brother will tell you what to do with the third part.'

In the end, there was to be no cremation or urn. Nor was there a home, a field or an oak tree. No brother survived to reveal the last part of her will. It is for those of us who live in peaceful times, and in safer places, to commemorate Sabina Spielrein, her daughters Renata and Eva, and her brothers Isaac, Jan and Emil. In the words that her grandfather Rabbi Mark Lublinsky would have said of the dead: *zichronam l'vrachah*. Let their memory be for a blessing.

FIFTEEN

Worlds apart

It is exactly a hundred years – almost to the day as I write this – since Sabina Spielrein presented her paper on 'Destruction as the Cause of Coming into Being' to the Vienna Psychoanalytic Society. The time has come to review what she said, and to honor her ideas in the light of what we know now about the biology of sexual reproduction, human psychology, and the connections between the two. I believe there is enough in her theory to indicate that she understood something that looks remarkably like the core of twenty-first century evolutionary thinking.

In the century since Spielrein's address, the worlds of both evolutionary studies and the talking treatments have expanded vastly. Whole scientific disciplines have arisen based on evolutionary theory: these include evolutionary biology, evolutionary psychology, evolutionary anthropology and evolutionary ecology. Scholars from these fields have examined everything from molecular genetics to gift-giving and religious practices in different cultures, all through the lens of evolution. Meanwhile the talking cure has given rise to uncountable schools of thought and methods of practice worldwide, not only in psychoanalysis but also psychotherapy, counseling, coaching and a whole range of similar professions. Yet the gulf between the two world views remains wide.

In one of these worlds, there are biological scientists who regard Freud's theories as self-referential, and unrelated to any recognizable biological principles. They have shown little interest in trying to apply their ideas to the talking cure. In the other world, there have been psychoanalysts, therapists and counselors who consider biology to be hopelessly deterministic, leading people to see genes as fate, and thus preventing them from taking charge of their own lives. People who offer talking treatments – from all the many different schools of thought – almost all go through their entire training without reading Darwin or receiving any grounding in basic evolutionary principles. For many of them, the whole idea of 'human nature' is something they reject as outdated and incorrect: they prefer to regard the human mind as a blank slate, affected only by individual experience.

Fortunately the debate has not been entirely polarized, and dialogue is now increasing. During the twentieth century there were visionary psychoanalysts like John Bowlby who tried to relate human feelings to some of the facts of biology, most especially the crucial attachment between mother and infant. There were inspired biologists like Gregory Bateson who showed a profound curiosity about the psychological therapies, and encouraged therapists to understand and apply evolutionary principles. In the last decade, a significant group of psychoanalysts, led by people like Peter Fonaghy and Mark Solms, have once again tried to harmonize psychoanalysis with the physiology and neurochemistry of the brain, which was where Freud originally started in the late nineteenth century.

These and many other researchers have started to build important bridges between the two worlds. However, nearly all of these attempts to reconnect the talking cure with biology have addressed what evolutionary scholars call 'proximal' causes – *how* things happen in biology. They haven't traced the workings of the mind back to 'distal' causes – looking at *why* behaviour and feelings contribute to reproduction and hence gene replication. In the view of even the most sympathetic evolutionists, the talking cure still awaits a coherent and persuasive theoretical underpinning in biology. Meanwhile, practitioners of the talking cure are not exactly clamoring for one.

They should be. Like any other account of how we feel and behave the way we do, evolutionary explanations add an extra dimension to our understanding of ourselves. As the evolutionary scholar Brian Boyd points out: 'Psychology and the social sciences are full of unconnected minitheories or empirical findings with no theoretical framework, which an evolutionary psychology could supply. Evolutionary psychology can ask...questions all too often ignored in earlier psychology. Why do we have this mental bias, or this behavior? Why has it been advantageous enough to become established in the species?...Some of the answers proposed in an evolutionary explanation of human nature may be premature, but they will be tested, sifted, and refined in due course. But incorporating deep time into our knowledge of the species adds a dimension whose absence had distorted all our thinking.'

In spite of the misconceptions held by many practitioners of the talking treatments, explanations of human behaviour based on our genetic or biological past do not deprive people of the opportunity to make choices. In a book entitled 'Sense and Nonsense: Evolutionary Perspective on Human Behaviour', Kevin Laland and Gillian Brown point out the following: 'Using evolutionary theory is not the same as taking a genetic determinist viewpoint. Genetic determinism is the belief that our genes contain blueprints for our behaviour that will always be followed and that constitute our destiny. Such a belief would run contrary to much that is known about how human behaviour develops. Where researchers talk about genetic influences on human behaviour, they do not mean that the behaviour is completely determined by genetic effects, that no other factors play a part in our development, or that a single gene is responsible for each behaviour. Although most evolutionary biologists focus exclusively on genetic inheritance, it does not follow that genes are the sole determinant of human behaviour, and the vast majority take it for granted that multiple environmental influences will play a part throughout development.'

In the same book, Laland and Brown take readers honestly through the various forms of evolutionary beliefs that have unfairly brought evolutionary thinking into disrepute in the past. These include Social Darwinism, which gave birth to the monsters of racism, eugenics and Nazism. They also included 'sociobiological' theories that claimed, for example, that violence was ineradicable in human beings, or that the role of homosexuals was to perform a 'helper' function in human groups. 'Sense and Nonsense' shows quite how irrational and discreditable such approaches to evolution actually are.

The implications of the contemporary approach to evolution are clear. If practitioners of the talking treatments want to be taken seriously in the twenty-first century, or to develop further, they can no longer exclude an evolutionary framework for the work they do. A re-evaluation of Spielrein's ideas would be good place to start. It would represent a return to the historical moment when biology and the talking cure parted company – and a way of reclaiming scientific legitimacy for the talking cure itself. It would heal a rift that was unnecessary in the first place, and has persisted for far too long.

Sabina Spielrein made an honorable attempt in 1911 to formulate a biological theory of how the mind worked, and she offered a way of underpinning the talking cure in biological principles. Her theory had some significant failings, but she also said some accurate and highly important things on the way, and it is now worth revisiting these. To offer an analogy, if Einstein had understood everything he needed to construct a viable theory of relativity, but had mistakenly worked out the conclusion that $e=mc \times 42$, people would not have completely dismissed or forgotten him. They would have retraced the steps of his logic and, sooner or later, reached the correct answer. If we now examine Spielrein's theory from this perspective, we find that she offered some principles that deserved serious consideration, and take us to the heart of modern biological thinking.

SIXTEEN

Destruction in creation's service

In Chapter Six I identified three crucial biological propositions in Spielrein's paper:

1. Reproduction predominates over survival.

2. Sex is a form of invasion, leading to the destruction of genes from both partners in the reconstitution of new life.

3. Human feelings correspond with the biological facts of reproduction.

In this chapter and the two following ones I want to look at each of these propositions in turn, through the eyes of modern biology and evolutionary studies. I intend to show how each proposition has been vindicated. In the final chapter I will describe how evolutionary approaches have finally been taken up by a small minority of psychoanalysts and therapists.

1. Reproduction predominates over survival.

It would be no exaggeration to say that this single idea now dominates biology and evolutionary theory in the twenty-first century. Spielrein stated the principle lyrically: 'The individual must strongly hunger for this new creation in order to place its own destruction in creation's service.' Modern thinkers would put it more succinctly: genes are selfish.

Selfish gene theory emerged gradually in the second half of the twentieth century through the work of people like Bill Hamilton, John Maynard Smith and George Williams, although it has become mostly associated with the name of Richard Dawkins. Dawkins is the first to admit that the term 'selfish gene' may not be the best description of how genes work, since it carries unnecessary overtones of moral judgment. Genes are not selfish in the sense of deciding how to behave. They simply do what they do, which is to replicate themselves, survive, and then replicate again. Even though Dawkins has never suggested this as alternative term, the 'dedicated duplicator' might be a better one than the selfish gene. The notion of the selfish gene has now supplanted Darwin's emphasis on the preservation of the species in modern evolutionary theory, although the rest of his thinking about natural and sexual selection remains largely intact.

At the core of selfish gene theory is that idea that whole organisms are in essence merely the vehicles for gene replication. In the process of evolution, different genes compete with each other for effectiveness in their adaptability to the environment when a change occurs, or in their attractiveness in terms of sexual choice.

Selfish gene theory is now an accepted belief in biology. It is also counter-intuitive for most people, since we normally think of reproduction in terms of our own individual identity, rather than as conglomerations of genes or packages of DNA. Those who require more convincing and have never read Dawkins' works, especially 'The Selfish Gene', should do so. However, here is a succinct extract from that book. In it, he explains why we exist as individual organisms and not just as an undifferentiated soup of self-replicating and competing lengths of DNA:

'The success that a replicator has in the world will depend on what kind of world it is – the pre-existing conditions. Among the most important of these conditions will be other replicators and their consequences…At some point in the evolution of life on our earth, this ganging up of mutually compatible replicators began to be formalized in the creation of distinct vehicles – cells, and later, many-celled bodies…This packaging of living material into discrete vehicles became such a salient and dominant feature that, when biologists arrived on the scene and started to ask questions about life, their questions were mostly about vehicles – individual organisms…It requires a deliberate mental effort to turn biology the right way up again, and remind ourselves that the replicators come first, in importance as well as history.'

One problematical aspect of the term 'selfish gene' is that it appears to carry the implication that genes never collaborate, and hence individuals do not do so either. It leads people to associate selfish gene theory with a view of nature as 'red in tooth and claw'. Nothing could be further from the truth. A large proportion of what is now called 'neo-Darwinist' thinking has been devoted to examining why conflict is so often absent in relationships, and co-operation such a common feature of animal and human life. As Dawkins points out, genes would stand little change of replicating themselves unless they could work together to further their own interests. Genes have to co-operate to build organisms, organisms have to co-operate to survive and live. In many species including humans, co-operation is also crucial for raising children and for social functioning generally.

For example, the most influential theorist of 'neo-Darwinism', Bill Hamilton, argued that looking after close relatives can promote ones own genes indirectly – so-called 'kin selection'. We can invest in all kinds of ways in our grandchildren, cousins and other relatives. Another great evolutionary scholar, Robert Trivers, has devoted much of his career to showing how mutual acts of generosity can help to perpetuate each person's genes: so-called 'reciprocal altruism'. In a similar way, the anthropologist Sarah Hrdy has proposed, in 'Mothers and Others' that humans are co-operative breeders, with communal child care as the norm in many human societies.

In modern biology, collaboration and generosity do not invalidate the idea of the selfish gene, they actually reinforce it. Taking a 'gene's-eye view' doesn't mean that only the gene itself ever benefits. Indeed, in the view of evolutionary anthropologists, our clans, lineage, faith communities or even the state may do well as a result of what our genes do. From an evolutionary perspective, everything that we collectively hand down to our offspring – including material wealth, moral codes, laws and rituals – enhances their genetic inheritance, and makes sure that this genetic inheritance has the best chance of prevailing in the long term.

What selfish gene theory offers, however, is an account that completely confirms Spielrein's understanding of the difference between the destiny of individual human beings and that of their genes. As she already knew, each sperm or egg carries a combination of its ancestors' genes, but selected randomly, like dealing a hand of playing cards after shuffling them. If any particular combination is robust enough to combine in an embryo, those genes will almost certainly outlive both the father and the mother. Although their role as parents will need to continue in order to provide food, shelter and protection and much more for the new offspring, in time there will be a stage when their deaths will become not only inevitable but – in an evolutionary sense – *desirable*. It will free up resources so that the genes that survive can have more living space, more resources, and hence more opportunities to replicate in their turn.

From the perspective of selfish gene theory, the question of why human beings get old and die should be turned on its head. The real explanation lies in the corollary: young people, generally speaking, rarely die. This is because the more deadly genes that we carry, and that will see all of us off, are counteracted by protective genes that keep them at bay until we have done our reproductive duty – or at least had a decent chance of doing so. If these protective genes were more effective and operated over a longer period of the life cycle, they would leave the world cluttered up with individuals past their reproductive potential. Protective and degenerative genes have evolved in tandem to keep the balance between sex and death at just the right level for both to stand the best chance of replication – but for themselves, not for us as individuals.

There is one further twist to the story of sex and death. Simple non-sexual organisms like bacteria do not die of their own accord, but only when their environment changes, for example through loss of sufficient water. Some biologists now believe that sexual reproduction and programmed cell death may have arrived at the same moment in evolutionary history, and complemented each other. It would be nice to try and connect this with Spielrein's notion that we have intimations of mortality during orgasm, and to suggest that this is an atavistic memory of that moment. However such thinking would be mystical rather than scientific. Evolutionists see drives as directed towards future chances of reproduction, and not looking backward to historical processes. Yet it is a striking fact that the arrival of inevitable death in our evolutionary past may have brought with it the consequence that Spielrein described – the need to surrender our genes into a destructive and reconstructive embrace during sex.

Although our minds may not be dwelling on death at the moment of sexual consummation as Spielrein believed, human beings have of course been aware since the birth of intelligence that we all die, and that the only way of leaving anything permanent behind us is to have sex. That is not always the conscious reason why we do so, but it is the reason all the same. It is the inevitability of death that accounts for the irresistibility of sex.

Spielrein wrote: *'The individual must strongly hunger for this new creation in order to place its own destruction in creation's service.'*

Modern evolutionary theory says: *'The imperative for all living organisms is the replication of their genes by direct or indirect means in the face of individual extinction.'*

SEVENTEEN

Unfamiliar intruders

The next principle I identified as crucial in Spielrein's theory was that *sex is a form of invasion, leading to the destruction of genes from both partners in the reconstitution of new life.*

For the first billion years of life on earth, sex didn't exist. Organisms reproduced simply by splitting in two. The vast majority of organisms still continue to reproduce in the same way. Strange as it may seem, no-one is entirely sure why sex evolved. Darwin thought it must be the best way of producing variations and therefore the widest range of possibilities for survival in a changing environment. However in this instance Darwin was wrong. You do not need sex to produce variation: it happens anyway as a result of cosmic radiation and errors of DNA copying. John Maynard Smith argued that it was incomprehensible why any female should want to 'chuck away' half her DNA. Whatever the reason for sex, he pointed out, it must have been a highly compelling one.

There are various current theories about why sex evolved and still continues in existence. These rejoice in wonderful names like Muller's ratchet, Kondrashov's hatchet, and Red Queen theory (names after the character in Alice in Wonderland who perpetually runs very fast without getting anywhere as the landscape runs with her.) The last of these theories is based on the idea that sex is part of a continual race to outwit hostile germs. Nowadays it is considered the most likely explanation of sex. What all these theories share, however, is a recognition that sex is an enormous genetic compromise for both parties and involves as much competition between the sexes as it does co-operation. Biologically speaking, it appears to be poised half way between invasion and alliance, parasitism and collaboration, or genetic rape and informed consent.

Just as genes are selfish, so too is sex. Both males and females promote their own genes however they can. This is not a moral judgment, nor a way of suggesting that the males and females of each species get together and consciously decide on a way of outwitting the opposite sex. It simply means that males are under constant biological pressure to find ways of making sure that their own genes prosper, while females are under similar pressure to do the same. The strategies that work best are then passed on to the next generation and are re-selected as successful in the next generation as well.

Darwin reckoned that sexual success depended on 'the ardor of the male' and the 'will of the female'. Some biologists nowadays argue that there is a third element as well: conflict between the evolutionary interests of the two sexes. There are many examples of how this operates. The most obvious is the one stated by Spielrein: a sperm quite literally invades an egg by burrowing through its relatively tough outer lining, using chemical means to do so. The main thing missing from her account is that the female fights this invasion just as aggressively as the male pursues it.

For example, after intercourse, an overwhelming majority of a man's sperm are destroyed in the woman's vagina or cervix by a variety of chemical processes. Almost certainly this process selects only the hardiest specimens for survival. If one or two succeed in the perilous journey of entering the woman's womb, making their way up the ovarian tubes, penetrating an egg and then conceiving an embryo, some of their genes will still be stripped away, in favour of genes from the egg itself. Strikingly, all DNA within the mitochondrion – the so-called powerhouse of every cell – is female, passed down only from the mother to her sons as well as her daughters, as mitochondrial DNA from the father is discarded.

Even when a pregnancy is established, there is still more than a fifty per cent chance that the woman's body will reject the resulting combination of her own genes with the ones from the selected sperm as unsuitable, and hence miscarry. Taken together, these processes ensure that a woman will only invest the effort of pregnancy *if* she has first made sure that there is more of her own DNA present in the embryo, and *if* the combined sets of genes will make for strong enough progeny to keep those genes going.

However once a pregnancy has started, the male genes fight back. Perhaps the most remarkable example of competition between male and female genes takes place in the placenta, which is entirely constructed by the father's genome. Robert Trivers has described the placenta as 'a ruthless parasitic organ existing solely for the maintenance and protection of the fetus, perhaps too often to the disregard of the maternal organism'. There is a hormonal battle during pregnancy, with genes from the male parent and those from the female competing with each other to determine the baby's size at birth. While genes from the father are busily promoting fetal growth hormone to produce a large and healthy baby, genes from the mother will be competing to restrict growth, in order to preserve the mother's energy and protect her from the risks of a difficult birth. Meanwhile the fetus itself will be striving to control the mother's physiology in different ways – including raising her insulin production and blood pressure – to get the best nutrition, and hence invest in its own unique genome.

In the light of such biological understanding, Spielrein's use of descriptions like 'force' and 'intrusion' seem highly accurate. One of the world's leading researchers into the workings of the placenta, David Haig from Harvard University, has described this struggle as a model of genetic conflict. He uses metaphors like 'at the front', 'behind the lines' and 'putting up resistance'. A number of other researchers have proposed that the battle continues beyond birth, with parts of the brain that have been programmed by paternal genes competing with the parts derived from maternal ones. There is, for example, evidence that genes from the mother play a leading role in constructing the cortex of the brain, while the father's genome takes control of the inner parts of the brain that are responsible for the emotions.

Conflict between the interests of male and female genes continues, of course, way beyond pregnancy and childhood, and is also expressed in the way that adults behave towards each other. In the words of the evolutionary psychologist David Buss: 'Those in our evolutionary past who failed to mate successfully failed to become our ancestors. All of us descend from a long and unbroken line of ancestors who competed successfully for desirable mates...We carry in us the sexual legacy of these success stories'. Another point that Buss makes is that these strategies are largely unconscious: 'Sexual strategies do not require conscious planning or awareness. Our sweat glands are 'strategies' for accomplishing the role of thermal regulation, but they require neither conscious planning nor awareness of the goal. Indeed, just as a piano player's sudden awareness of her hands may impede performance, most human sexual strategies are best carried out without the awareness of the actor.'

As Spielrein wrote in her early diaries, reproductive sex involves a conflict of interests between males and females. This exactly reflects the interests of egg-carriers and sperm-carriers just as it does in every other species. One episode of sexual intercourse requires little investment by a man, but will potentially lead to a nine-month pregnancy followed by up to two decades of child-rearing by a woman. It is not surprising that – across all cultures – men largely desire youth, beauty and variety, while women largely desire strength, economic and social status, and a capacity for commitment. Conflicts between the sexes are the social rule, not the exception. They include arguments over the initiation of sex during courtship, bickering over money and commitment in marriages, separation and divorce. In every culture, exaggeration and deception are practiced in order to achieve extra-marital couplings. Many evolutionary psychologists now believe that sexual preferences like homosexuality are not as 'non-reproductive' as they seem. A majority of those practicing gay or lesbian sex may actually conceive children through heterosexual encounters in the course of their lives, while bisexuality may even confer some advantages in terms of the signals it offers to the opposite sex. It is possible that people with masochistic tendencies like Spielrein are using a sexual strategy that makes similar sense in reproductive terms.

There are also universal differences between men and women in the way that sexual power is enacted. These include male sexual harassment in private or public, and serious sexual assault on women – including the huge incidence of rape that takes place during war. In virtually every culture, there is female prostitution, a preference for male children – whose lifetime potential for gene replication is much higher – and often a higher rate of infanticide or feticide of females. All these things can be understood in terms of evolved mating strategies for gene replication: what men and women feel and desire is not the same.

In his book 'The Evolution of Desire', David Buss writes: 'Wishes and denials will not make psychological differences disappear, any more than they will make beard growth or breast development disappear. Harmony between men and women will be approached only when these denials are swept away and we squarely confront the differing desires of each sex.'

Spielrein wrote in her diary as a medical student: 'We must not forget the fundamental difference between man and woman. Man wants to embrace, woman prefers to be embraced...Woman is more discriminating in her choice because it is more difficult to find a personality that fits the ideal: it is for these reasons that the woman is generally monogamous, when she truly loves; for opposite reasons, the man is less discriminating and more or less polygamous.' Whether or not one agrees with such a broad characterization, there is no doubt that men and women have different reproductive objectives, and correspondingly different strategies that reflect conflict as much as co-operation.

Spielrein described sex as a process of destruction and reconstruction at every level: *'a union in which one forces its way into the other.'*

Modern evolutionary theory says: *'As well as co-operation, sexual reproduction involves inherent conflict at every level between male and female genetic interests.'*

EIGHTEEN

Corresponding feelings

The third crucial principle of Spielrein's argument was that *human feelings correspond with the biological facts of reproduction.*

There is only one idea in modern evolutionary biology that has gained a status almost as central as the selfish gene. It is 'reproductive fitness.' Emotions play an absolutely central part in what enables us to achieve this.

Just as Darwin used the term 'fit' to mean 'fitting the surrounding environment', biologists now use the phrase reproductive fitness to mean the capacity to leave surviving progeny behind at one's death. Reproductive fitness can only be a retrospective judgment: we may be athletically strong, and have many children and grandchildren, but if none of the great-grandchildren are equipped to survive, then our genes will have proved unfit. All that we can do is to procreate, protect the interests of the next generation and then, as it were, keep our posthumous fingers crossed.

One of the best accounts of reproductive fitness is by the evolutionary anthropologist James Chisholm. In a book with the wonderful title 'Death, Hope and Sex.' Chisholm puts together a extraordinary jigsaw of developmental psychology, cultural studies, and evolutionary theory. He shows how all aspects of human endeavor, from child rearing to faith systems and moral law, and especially the expression of our emotions, point in the same direction. Without of course being aware of Spielrein, he affirms her objection to Freud's emphasis on pleasure: 'People, like all organisms,' he writes, 'are not evolved to maximize health, wealth, happiness, life span, vigor, power, prestige, beauty, love, sex, truth, honor, reason or anything else, but to have descendants, which is continuation'.

Our whole range of mental, psychological, behavioral, parental and moral strategies, Chisholm proposes, are ultimately geared towards continuity. He talks of childhood development as something that has evolved to equip us for later reproduction as adults, and discusses how it has been shaped to meet that purpose. In doing so, he confirms the idea that Spielrein put forward in one of her letters to Jung. ('To express my own opinion', she wrote, 'I would include the instinct for self-preservation in the instinct for preservation of the species.) He describes how we use our own 'theory of mind' to observe our own thoughts and feelings, interpret those of other people, and make judgments based on our conclusions.

Most significantly, Chisholm summarizes how modern evolutionary thinking offers a view of emotions as our best way – indeed our only way – of assessing our interactions with others and with the environment, and how far these are progressing our reproductive interests. He equates emotions with rational decision-making or (in evolutionary language) 'trade-offs' between the advantages of one action and another. He argues that emotions like fear and love are our ways of checking the balance between risk and opportunity at any given moment. He writes: 'To achieve long term fitness, organisms must always first avoid short-term disaster: they must avoid dangerous cliffs. Once they have achieved a degree of security, however, they can afford to invest in the future: they can set the stage for long-term fitness projects...What we call love is *value experience*, which ultimately is the representation of ...the interactive contingencies that determine reproductive value.'

Chisholm analyses how human beings try to maximise their chances of gene replication, using their emotions to do so. If the biological purpose of being human is to create more humans, he points out, all adults will have to make continual decisions about the trade-off between seeking to procreate here and now, or delaying it until later. At any moment, he suggests, sex represents an irresistible opportunity because it will create progeny who may outlive us if we die tomorrow (hence the urgency of sexual desire). At the same time, it represents a threat because having children now may lead to a depletion of resources for the parents and a risk to their survival (hence the anxiety that surrounds the desire). This is especially the case for their mothers, who will have to nourish and look after them for years to come.

Chisholm points out there is another aspect to this dilemma. Having lots of babies with lots of partners as soon as possible may pay off in the short run in terms of numbers; but at the same time it may take its toll on one or both parents, so that in the end the health and lives of all the family are put at risk. It will also create other risks for both sexes, including same sex-rivalry and social exclusion. He looks at different kinds of parent-child attachment, pair mating and family make-up, and sees these as evolutionary variations.

Fascinatingly, he shows how human beings in conditions of relative deprivation pursue sex urgently soon after puberty and have many children. By contrast, where both parents and children live in more secure conditions, adults will tend to wait longer before conceiving, and will invest their resources in a smaller number of children. They will invest indirectly in their genes through educating their children and leaving them large bequests, or putting their energy into their wider family, communities or even nations.

This way of bringing together modern evolutionary thinking with developmental and sexual psychology, offers confirmation of Spielrein's general approach. His work provides support for her assertion that sexual desire is inherently ambivalent: it involves both a biological imperative and an assessment of risk. Orgasm may not be destroying our individuality, as Spielrein had believed, nor do we actually become apprehensive of death as a climax occurs. However, our genes have limited chances of continuation, and we constantly have to balance our desire against the risks of genetic extinction. Our feelings are therefore continually telling us what we need to know about the consignment of our precious genes to a reconstruction with someone else's, and whether it has all been worth it. Feelings of resistance are our best guide to the risks of desire and the avoidance of genetic extinction through making the wrong choices.

As Spielrein suggested, our emotions represent the facts of reproduction. Feelings are our way of assessing *when* we have sex, *how often* we have it, and *with whom*. The 'joyful feeling of coming into being' represents hope for continuation. The 'resistance, anxiety, and disgust' that Spielrein described, represent the fear that we may have chosen the wrong trade-off: the wrong time, or the wrong partner. The proportions of joy and anxiety surrounding each consummation will logically equate with the balance of opportunity and risk felt by the individual at the time. Arguably, feelings of hope and danger – particularly for women – will be more acute at that time that at any other. The emotions will also be magnified or diminished by whatever expectations the person brings from their own personality and history.

Chisholm's line of thinking helps us to understand both the weaknesses of Spielrein's argument and also its strengths. One of its main weaknesses was that she believed sexual let-down was a universal experience, and she drew her conclusions from that belief. With hindsight, we can see that her own personal history and sexuality may have inclined her to hold such a belief. Any victim of emotional and physical abuse like her would be more likely to seek urgent comfort from sex, to take risks, to feel intense anxiety before each liaison, and then be disappointed afterwards. For a young, medical student like Spielrein, feelings of both joy and resistance might be at their height before and after sex with a highly desirable partner like Jung (with high status, intelligence and strength) in a situation of great risk. All these factors may have given her an acute insight into the tensions inherent in sexual reproduction, but they may also have led her to assume that her feelings and experiences were more universal than they actually are.

Most important of all, this perspective finally offers us a way of reformulating Spielrein's argument. *In modern evolutionary thinking, the idea that we experience a tension between 'sex versus survival' makes perfect sense.* However, the cause of our anxiety about sex isn't that we are poised on the cusp between conception and death at the moment of orgasm, or because the reproductive drive has a destructive component. It is because we are making judgments, at every moment of our adult lives, about how much to invest in direct and indirect ways in the perpetuation of our genes, and how much in avoiding risks that will imperil ourselves, or our existing and potential genetic succession. In other words, we are always balancing our wish to reproduce, not against the *immediate* risk of extinction as Spielrein deduced, but against *potential future* ones.

Ultimately our emotions at any moment – especially concerning the act of sex itself – represent those judgments.

Spielrein wrote: *'It would be highly unlikely if the individual did not at least surmise, through corresponding feelings, these internal deconstructive-reconstructive events.'*

Modern evolutionary theory says: *'Our feelings correspond to the way we balance opportunities for genetic continuation against the risks of extinction.'*

NINETEEN

The talking cure reconstructed

In Chapter Fifteen I mentioned that a number of pioneers during the twentieth century followed Spielrein in trying to formulate a biological understanding of to the talking cure. In this final chapter I want to describe a small minority of contemporary thinkers who have tried to harmonize the talking cure with the fundamental principles of evolutionary theory.

They have done so not only by looking at the proximal questions about biology and the mind *(how does this work?)*, but at distal evolutionary causes *(why has this feeling or behavior succeeded in the struggle for selection?)*. In other words, they have been interested in finding out how our behaviour and feelings align with our principal biological purpose – continuation – and in applying this in their practical work with patients. Their writings show that finally, a century after this might have happened, practitioners of the talking cure have begun to follow the same evolutionary signposts that Spielrein identified.

In 2000 a group of sixteen psychologists and psychotherapists published a collection of essays entitled 'Genes on the Couch'. Edited by the British psychologist Paul Gilbert and his American colleague Kent Bailey, it brought together writers from a number of different mental health disciplines and theoretical orientations, including contemporary Freudians and Jungians. Collectively, they drew on ideas that have been emerging among influential evolutionary scholars during the previous twenty years, particularly in the United States. This includes major modern evolutionary thinkers like Leda Cosmides and John Tooby in California, and Randolph Nesse from the University of Michigan.

The contributors to 'Genes on the Couch' share certain fundamental beliefs that link them directly to Darwin himself. They all accept as an important truth the idea that we are evolved creatures, with evolved behaviour, and evolved strategies for reproduction. They recognize that we need an understanding of evolution not just to make sense of human psychology, but as a starting point for any treatment of mental distress. They are all unified by their wish to understand fundamental human emotions such as desire, anxiety, fear, rage and jealousy as serving evolutionary purposes.

In an introduction to 'Genes on the Couch', the editors recall Darwin in talking about rivalry between members of the same sex, and rivalry between members of the opposite sexes. Following modern evolutionary thinking, they assume that we all possess certain evolved psychological programs that set the broad shape of how we might behave in any given situation, but without rigidly prescribing the exact response that we might choose. In common with Bowlby, they accept that some of these programs may have evolved very long ago in environments that were so different from our own that they are no longer useful.

In an echo of Spielrein, they recognize that our evolved strategies for survival and reproduction do not necessarily all follow the same pattern, and their aims may not even be compatible. They identify the function of all painful mental states as being to alert us to dangers, threats and losses. They argue that the aim of talking treatments should be to help people understand the evolutionary nature of these dangers, threats and losses and why the distress caused by them can be so intense.

One particularly interesting contribution to the book comes from the Jungian analyst Anthony Stevens. He offers a sympathetic account of Jung's evolutionary thought. Stevens proposes that it would be better to reject Jung's rather mystical notion of the 'collective unconscious' as a source of powerful images and myths, and to talk instead about how some psychological programs are shared across the whole human species – like the tendency to idealize the image of the perfect woman or perfect man. Stevens also suggests that we should see Jung's idea of mental 'complexes', such as the so-called 'inferiority complex', as being formed from entirely healthy psychological units, each serving different strategic purposes in the business of survival and reproduction.

Anthony Stevens previously authored a book, along with John Price, examining the origins of mental disorders. It is called

'Evolutionary Psychiatry.' Like his essay in 'Genes on the Couch', the book is a significant attempt to build a bridge between modern Jungian psychology and evolution. He doesn't mention Spielrein in either work. However what he writes helps us imagine how Spielrein in her own mind might have taken some of Jung's ideas and developed them in the way she did. Stevens' line of thinking also points in an intriguing direction: that the programs directed at promoting survival and those necessary for procreation occupy different networks within the brain, and may sometimes be in competition with each other. The work of neuroscientists like Jaak Panksepp and Antonio Damasio suggest that this is indeed the case. This offers more support for Spielrein's view of the tensions inherent in reproduction.

However, for reassessing Spielrein's ideas, by far the most relevant essay in 'Genes on the Couch' comes from an American psychoanalyst named Daniel Kriegman. In a compelling metaphor (and a particularly courageous one for a practicing psychoanalyst) Kriegman talks of the need to rediscover the evolutionary baby in the bathwater of psychoanalysis. 'Before we empty the enormous quantity of dirty bathwater', Kriegman writes, 'wouldn't we be wise to make a search to see if there is a baby in it? Not only would I suggest that we will find a living baby, I would also suggest that the baby has nearly drowned and is in desperate need of evolutionary biological resuscitation'. Kriegman goes on to describe how psychoanalysis has effectively become shrunken to an analysis of the relationship between therapist and patient in the consulting room. 'All too often,' he writes 'psychoanalytic treatment – operating outside the context of a valid scientific view of human nature – is now dominated by strained, at times untenable, interpretations about relationships'.

Kriegman sets out a much fuller version of this argument in an earlier book: 'The Adaptive Psyche', written with his colleague Malcolm Slavin. What that book proposes is no less than a total reinterpretation of psychoanalysis in order to harmonize it, as Freud had originally intended, with Darwin's core ideas. In 'The Adaptive Psyche', Slavin and Kriegman acknowledge that Freud's view of the evolutionary process was 'in some ways quite crude and quaint'. They make clear their belief that Freud lacked an accurate conception of natural selection; he intuitively sensed, but could not conceptualize, an understanding of the link between the experiences of our ancestors and the evolved design of the modern human psyche. Yet far from dismissing Freud's work out of hand on account of this, they argue that Freud's 'flawed yet appropriate efforts to deal with the overall structure of the psyche within an adaptive context might still be rescued within a world of modern evolutionary theory that has moved dramatically beyond Freud's limited picture of it.'

Slavin and Kriegman touch in tantalizing ways on some similar themes to Spielrein. They talk of the long, dismal history of attempts to distance human psychology from the rest of nature. They suggest that the emphasis on culture (or language, morality, religion, curiosity, etc) is a defensive way of separating humans from the rest of the animal world. Drawing on the work of evolutionary theorists like Robert Trivers and Bill Hamilton, they speak of the ample evidence that now exists that organisms, throughout nature, are adept at detecting not only kin but exact degrees of kinship, thus emphasizing our intuitive drive to replicate our own genes.

In examining the relationship between parents and their offspring, they assert that conflict between parents and children isn't just a matter of the children's crude, untutored biology resisting the parents' attempts to socialize them. Crucially, it can also be viewed as a biological conflict between differing needs of the two generations. They point out that the design of the child psyche has been fashioned by hundreds of thousands of generations of such conflicts. On virtually every psychological issue in the course of human development, they argue, an evolutionarily successful way of being a parent entails a divided strategy: to treat any child both as an ally but also as a competitor.

Very much of the case laid out by Slavin and Kriegman depends on this idea of the conflict between one generation and the next. We are driven to replicate, but the children we have succeed in conceiving no longer represent our own interests. 'A self designed for the human relational world must be prepared to engage in an extraordinarily complex set of developmental strategies that serve, in part, to defend against having one's interest usurped by others.'

In a remarkable conclusion, Slavin and Kriegman propose that 'we are essentially semi-social beings whose nature or self-structure and motivational system is inherently divided between the two eternally conflicting aims (i.e. survival and reproduction)'. Interestingly, they focus almost entirely on the relationship between the generations and have little to say about gender relations. Although they emphasise with clarity the tension between individual survival and gene replication, and between one generation and the next, they do not explicitly endorse Spielrein's view that this tension operates between the sexes.

This is a puzzling gap in their work, and indeed in the work of evolutionary psychotherapists generally. In the words of Richard Dawkins: 'If there is conflict of interests between parents and children, who share fifty per cent of each other's genes, how much more severe must be the conflict between mates, who are not related to each other?' It would be a relatively small step for the evolutionary psychotherapists who have focussed on the tensions between parent and child to turn their attention to those between parent and parent.

Having said that, Slavin and Kriegman do offer one striking insight that remind us of Spielrein and Jung. In 'The Adaptive Psyche', they insist on the necessity for therapists to be aware of their own evolutionary interests when seeing patients, not least where the therapist is a heterosexual male and the patient an attractive younger woman. In Kriegman's essay in 'Genes on the Couch', he points out how generations of sexist male therapists have persecuted female patients by accusing them of behaving seductively or provocatively, when they have done no more than dress and behave in ways that evolutionary imperatives have determined. He argues that female display is natural in order to promote their own reproductive interests, and criticizes male therapists who are only too ready to blame women patients for the normal male biological response that they are inevitably stimulating.

This narrative, of course, bears an uncanny resemblance to the very encounter between Jung and Spielrein that led to her view of the nature of the biological relations between the two sexes. 'The Adaptive Psyche' brings us full circle. It shows how psychoanalysis has, finally, acquired enough *biological* insight to make amends for the double injustice done to Sabina Spielrein: pathologising the victim, and ignoring her ground-breaking ideas.

Psychoanalysts, therapists and counselors now need to redress the injustice done to Spielrein both as a woman and a thinker. They need to join with the modern inheritors of her genius to reconstruct a theory of the talking cure that makes evolutionary and scientific sense. To adapt Daniel Kriegman's words, it would require letting out a very great deal of bathwater, and nurturing a very different kind of baby.

EPILOGUE

Sabina Spielrein tried to propose a biological theory of sex that could underpin the talking cure. She did not succeed. Whether she might have done so in time if her hearers had been more attentive, forgiving, collaborative, or simply better informed biologically, we will never know. What is certain is that she understood enough of the core principles of biology and its relation to psychology to take the most adventurous steps anyone had yet taken to harmonize them. I believe that qualifies her for the description of genius.

She understood the simple principle that lies at the centre of modern evolutionary theory. Biologically speaking, the purpose of our existence is to reproduce. Survival is at the service of reproduction. Our bodies and minds have evolved in order to survive in the ways that will best serve our reproductive interests. The trade-offs we make – particularly the choices we make at any moment about whether to invest in survival or reproduction – are all made ultimately in the long-term interests of reproduction.

Spielrein also understood that the unconscious is an evolutionary unconscious: it drives us at every stage to serve the purposes of evolution – to survive and to procreate, in anticipation of our own individual deaths. The talking cure needs to take into account our intuitive knowledge of these facts, and the feelings that represent them.

I have tried in *Sex versus Survival* to offer a balanced picture of Sabina Spielrein's life, and of her strengths and weaknesses as a scientific thinker. I have not attempted to provide a full biological or evolutionary account of how we might reframe 'the talking cure' in Darwinian terms. Such an account would need to incorporate the principles of variation, natural selection and sexual selection. It would have to encompass co-operation as well as conflict, and to look at how these are expressed across the life cycle between males and females, between parents and children, and within groups.

Above all, it would need to offer explanations of how the imperatives of reproductive fitness and gene replication are reflected in the human mind, its variations, its troubles, and its receptiveness to healing. Such a project is long overdue, but it is vastly too ambitious for here, for now, or for myself. If in this short book I have helped to commemorate and honor Sabina Spielrein, it is enough.

APPENDIX

Spielrein's 'Biological facts' in paraphrase (see Chapter Six)

'During sex, an egg and a sperm unite. In the process, each of them is destroyed as a single cell. New life originates because of this destruction. Some species like the mayfly actually die during sex. The species survives but the individual adults are destroyed at the same time. Each individual carries such a strong wish for its species to survive that it is actually prepared to destroy itself to fulfil this wish.

'In more advanced species like human beings, the whole individual will obviously not be destroyed during the sexual act. However, the egg and sperm are not just ordinary cells like any other. They are intimately associated with the person's entire life. In a concentrated form, they contain the power of reproduction. This influences not only their own development as cells. It also influences the development of the whole person. When fertilization takes place, it destroys these important substances.

'The fusion of egg and sperm during sex mirrors the physical act of sex itself. Both are forms of union in which one person (the male) forces his way into the other (the female). The difference between conception and sexual intercourse is merely one of scale. In each case, only a part of the individual is taken into the other, but in that instant the part represents the whole. In other words, the man forces his penis into the woman's vagina in the act of sexual intercourse, and the sperm forces its way into the egg in the conception of an embryo.

'At both levels, the male merges with the female. In both cases, the female takes on a new shape as a result of penetration by the unfamiliar intruder. An alteration comes over the couple during sex and the egg and sperm during conception. Destruction and reconstruction always go side by side, but in sex this all takes place very quickly. The individual expels the egg or sperm in the same rapid way that urine or feces are excreted.

'It is very hard to imagine that individuals do not have an intuitive feeling that both destruction and reconstruction are going on. That is why the joyful feeling of coming alive that is present in the sexual drive is also accompanied by a feeling of resistance, of anxiety or disgust. This is not because the genitals are close to the organs of excretion as some people have suggested. Nor is it because we feel negative about sexual desire because we have to renounce it so often, as Freud has proposed. It is because we instinctively sense that sex is destroying us as well as creating something new.'

FURTHER READING

Almost the only mention of Spielrein in the literature of early psychoanalysis appears in Freud's brief acknowledgement to her in a footnote to 'Beyond the Pleasure Principle' (in *The Standard Edition of the Complete Psychological Works of Sigmund Freud.* Translated by James Strachey. London, Hogarth Press, 1953-74). Her significant role in the relationship between Freud and Jung first became apparent after the publication of letters between the two men in 1974 (*The Freud/Jung Letters,* edited by William McGuire. London. Hogarth/Routledge and Kegan Paul, 1974).

There is no single compilation of all the surviving letters to and from Sabina Spielrein, nor of the different fragments of her diaries. What does exist is scattered over several volumes, sometimes with inaccurate dates or incomplete details of provenance. This is a significant handicap to scholarship. The bulk of Spielrein's letters and diaries were published by the Italian psychoanalyst Aldo Carotenuto, along with Freud's letters to her, and a short biographical sketch written from a mainly Jungian point of view (*A Secret Symmetry: Sabina Spielrein between Jung and Freud.* Aldo Carotenuto, translated by A. Pomerans, J. Shepley and K. Winston. New York, Pantheon, 1982.)

The material in that book has been supplemented by the publication of a more recent one, edited by two other Jungian analysts. (*Sabina Spielrein, Forgotten Pioneer of Psychoanalysis,* edited by Coline Covington and Barbara Wharton. Hove, Brunner-Routledge, 2003). This contains further extracts from Spielrein's diary, some of Jung's letters to her, her hospital records from the Burghölzli, Jung's original referral letter to Freud, and some further letters including ones between Spielrein and her mother. Other contributions include translations of several of Spielrein's papers (including *The Origins of the Words Papa and Mama*') and a wealth of informative essays from different perspectives by Johannes Cremerius, Bernard Minder, Angela Graf-Nold, Zvi Lothane, Sabine Richerbächer, Nicolle Kress-Rosen, Fernando Vidal and the two editors. None of these essays takes a biological standpoint, while one or two offer outrageous defenses of Jung's behaviour, and some fall into the error of pathologising both Spielrein and her theory. Nevertheless this book and Carotenuto's are essential reading for anyone who wants to know more about Spielrein.

There is also no standard edition of all Spielrein's published papers. However, the Journal of Analytical Psychology has helpfully published a number of these, translated into English. Her most important essay appeared there in its first English translation. (*Destruction as the cause of coming into being*. Sabina Spielrein, translated by Barbara Wharton. Journal of Analytical Psychology, 1994, **39**, 155-186). At the same time they published a helpful paper on psychoanalysis in Russia. (*How psychoanalysis was received in Russia*. Alexander Etkind. Journal of Analytical Psychology, 1994, **39**, 191-202). Since then, the journal has published several of her other essays in translation, and a helpful summary of the available information about Spielrein, particularly from her years in Russia. (*Love, psychoanalysis and destruction*. Victor Ovcharenko, translated by C.J Wharton. Journal of Analytical Psychology, 1999, **44**, 355-373.)

There is a sympathetic review of Spielrein's published papers by Adeline van Waning (*The works of pioneering psychoanalyst Sabina Spielrein*. Adeline van Waning, International Review of Psycho-Analysis, 1992, **19**, 399-413). Another essay is by Cifali (*Sabina Spielrein, a woman psychoanalyst: another picture*. Mireille Cifali. Journal of Analytical Psychology, 2001, **46**, 129-138). A more recent paper includes a bibliography of works by and about Spielrein, including novels, films and plays. (*Sabina Spielrein: a bibliography*. Brigitte Allain-Dupré. Journal of Analytical Psychology, 2004, **49**, 421-433.) The most thorough consideration of Spielrein's ideas from an orthodox modern psychoanalytical point of view is a chapter by Ron Britton (In: *Sex, Death and the Superego: Experiences in Psychoanalysis*. Ronald Britton. London, Karnac, 2003).

From the many other articles and more extended works written about Spielrein and the 'analytic triangle', the most incisive, fair and accurate is the one by Forrester and Appignanesi (*Freud's Women*. John Forrester and Lisa Appignanesi. London, Weidenfeld and Nicholson, 1992). The most comprehensive book about the relationships between the three protagonists is by John Kerr (*A Most Dangerous Method: The Story of Jung, Freud and Sabina Spielrein*.

John Kerr. New York, Knopf, 1993). His book contains a overwhelming amount of detail of how early psychoanalytic theory developed, but it has the unique merit of acknowledging Spielrein's originality and importance as a theorist. From the many biographies of Jung, I would recommend the one by Ronald Hayman (*A Life of Jung*. Ronald Hayman. London, Bloomsbury, 1999). Among the uncountable books written about Freud, the best remains the one by Peter Gay (*Freud, A Life for our Times*. Peter Gay. London, Dent, 1988).

For those interested in the history of evolutionary biology and psychology, a good overview is provided by Lois Magner. (*A History of the Life Sciences*. Lois Magner. 2nd edition, New York, Marcel Dekker, 1994) Anyone interested in theories of sexual psychology around the turn of the twentieth century should read the work of Frank Sulloway. (*Freud: Biologist of the Mind*. Frank Sulloway. London, Burnett, 1979). Although Sulloway makes no direct mention of Spielrein, his account of Freud's debt to biology, and of his determination to evade the debt, is compelling. Sulloway is not popular with Freudians, and those wanting to read a critique of his work from a psychoanalytic perspective should read Paul Robinson (*Freud and his Critics*. Paul Robinson. Berkeley, University of California Press, 1993.)

The best account of selfish gene theory appears in the works of Richard Dawkins (see in particular *The Selfish Gene*. Richard Dawkins. Oxford, Oxford University Press, 1976 and *The Ancestor's Tale*. Richard Dawkins. London, Weidenfeld and Nicholson, 2004.) One contemporary view of the biological relationship between sex and death is described in William R. Clark (*Sex and the Origins of Death*. William R. Clark. Oxford, Oxford University Press, 1996.) Good accounts of the evolutionary biology of sex appear in Matt Ridley's book on the 'Red Queen' theory and Olivia Judkins' wonderfully racy guide. (*The Red Queen: Sex and the Evolution of Human Nature*. Matt Ridley. London, Viking, 1993; *Dr Tatiana's Sex Guide to All Creation: the definitive guide to the evolutionary biology of sex*. Olivia Judkins. London, Chatto and Windus, 2002). A good antidote to evolutionary writing about conflict and competition is Martin Nowak's work on co-operation. (*Supercooperators: Evolution, Altruism and Human Behavior*. Martin Nowak with Roger Highfield. London, Canongate, 2011.)

Marlena Zuk offers a helpful feminist approach to the appropriate and inappropriate uses of evolutionary thinking in relation to human sexual psychology (*Sexual Selections: What we can and can't learn from animals*. Marlena Zuk. California, University of California, 2003). A key text covering scholarship relating to human sexuality is by David Buss (*The Evolution of Desire: Strategies of Human Mating*. David Buss. New York, Basic Books, revised edition 2003).

Gregory Bateson's main collection of writings appears in 'Steps to an Ecology of Mind' (Bateson G. *Steps to an Ecology of Mind*. New York, Ballantine, 1972). James Chisholm, has written an updated presentation of evolutionary ecology, arguing the case for evolutionary understanding as the basis for self-awareness (Chisholm J, *Death, Hope and Sex: Steps to an Evolutionary Ecology of Mind and Morality*. Cambridge, Cambridge University Press, 1999.) John Bowlby's work on attachment theory is reported in his main work *Attachment and Loss* (Bowlby J, *Attachment and Loss*. Volume 1. London, Hogarth, 1969; Volume 2. London, Hogarth, 1973). He also wrote his own biography of Darwin. (Bowlby, J. *Charles Darwin: A Biography*. London, Routledge, 1990.)

Among recent reformulations of psychotherapy taking account of modern evolutionary thinking, the most useful are 'The Adaptive Design of the Human Psyche' (*The Adaptive Design of the Human Psyche: Psychoanalysis,, Evolutionary Biology and the Therapeutic Process*. Malcolm Slavin and Daniel Kriegman. London, Guilford Press, 1992) and 'Genes on the Couch' (*Genes on the Couch: Explorations in evolutionary psychotherapy*. Edited by Paul Gilbert and Kent Bailey. London, Brunner-Routledge, 2000). Much of this work is based on ideas from Leah Cosmides and John Tooby, and from Randolph Nesse (see *The Adapted Mind: Evolutionary Psychology and the Generation of Culture*. Edited by L Cosmides , H Barrett H and J. Tooby. Oxford, Oxford University Press, 1992; *Why We Get Sick: the New Science of Darwinian Medicine*. R. Nesse and G. Williams. New York, Times Books, 1995.)

A good introduction to contemporary thinking about evolution appears in the opening chapters of Brian Boyd's book about the origin of stories. (*On the Origin of Stories: Evolution, Cognition and Fiction*. Brian Boyd. Harvard, Harvard University Press, 2009.) A useful short guide to evolutionary thinking is the book by Kevin

Laland and Gillian Brown (*Sense and Nonsense: Evolutionary Perspectives on Human Behavior*. K. Laland and G. Brown. Oxford, Oxford University Press, 2nd edition, 2011). For readers who want to advance their knowledge of evolution generally I would recommend the recent volume edited by Michael Muhlenbein (*Human Evolutionary Biology*. Edited by Michel Muhlenbein. Cambridge, Cambridge University Press, 2010).

ACKNOWLEDGEMENTS

Many people have helped me in direct or indirect ways to formulate the ideas in this book. Colleagues at the Tavistock Clinic in London have been kind enough to invite me to contribute every year to our annual management training event. It was there that I conceived of an imaginary 'Spielrein Institute', a kind of fantasy counterpart to the Tavistock itself. Although I originally did so in a jocular fashion, it led me in time to take a proper interest in the life and ideas of Sabina Spielrein, and hence to discover her genius. Sebastian Kraemer, for a long time my mentor at the Tavistock, has always encouraged me to go against the grain and to challenge every orthodoxy in the world of psychotherapy; he was supportive of this project as well. Three imaginative editors have had enough faith to allow me to explore in writing my ideas about evolution and psychotherapy. One is Ivan Eisler at the Journal of Family Therapy where I published an article entitled: 'Whatever happened to biology: reconnecting family therapy with its evolutionary roots'. Subsequently Christopher Martyn at the international medical journal 'QJM' and Fiona Moss at the Postgraduate Medical Journal have given me amazing license to use my regular columns on the world of ideas to promote unconventional views or tell unusual stories – including that of Sabina Spielrein – where other editors would have said no.

Conversations with Dave Bell from the British Psychoanalytic Society and Jim Hopkins from Kings College London have been helpful, although I do not think either of them would endorse my assessment of Spielrein's theory. I have benefitted from all the previous accounts of Sabina Spielrein, especially those by Aldo Carotenuto, John Kerr, John Forrester and Lisa Appignanesi, and Coline Covington and Barbara Wharton, and also from the many translations and discussions of her ideas in the Journal of Analytical Psychology and elsewhere. In the final stages of writing I have been extraordinarily fortunate to receive the support of two evolutionary scholars. Jim Chisholm from the University of Western Australia has been amazingly generous with his time and comments, particularly with his belief that I was definitely 'on to something'.

Daniela Sieff has offered valuable help by pointing out in a critical but friendly way where I was overstating my case or drawing unwarranted conclusions. However I am entirely happy to absolve all these people from any evolutionary, psychoanalytic or other errors that appear in this book. As Jung commented on Spielrein's ideas, these are 'home grown'.

Finally and most importantly, my family. Our children Ruth and David, have been ridiculously tolerant as always of my habit of getting bees in my bonnet and pursuing these selfishly by reading or writing when I should be doing more sociable and entertaining things. My wife, Lee Wax, has had faith in this project even at times when I lacked this myself. She has done everything from reading the emerging text, and editing it at every stage, to insisting that I explained the ideas out loud to make sure the case for Spielrein's ideas held water and was fair and reasonable. This book would not have appeared without her unstinting support and love. My deep gratitude, always.

Printed in Great Britain
by Amazon.co.uk, Ltd.,
Marston Gate.